THE THINKING STRATEGIST

THE THINKING STRATEGIST

Unleashing the Power of Strategic Management to Identify, Explore and Solve Problems, 2nd Edition

By

Vickie Cox Edmondson
University of Georgia, USA

AMERICAN MARKETING
ASSOCIATION

emerald
PUBLISHING

United Kingdom – North America – Japan
India – Malaysia – China

Emerald Publishing Limited
Howard House, Wagon Lane, Bingley BD16 1WA, UK

First edition 2018
Copyright © 2018 Emerald Publishing Limited

Second edition 2022
Copyright © 2022 Vickie Edmondson Foreword: © 2022 Jonas Robinson.
Published under exclusive licence by Emerald Publishing Limited

Reprints and permissions service
Contact: permissions@emeraldinsight.com

British Library Cataloguing in Publication Data
A catalogue record for this book is available from the British Library

ISBN: 978-1-80382-562-5 (Print)
ISBN: 978-1-80382-559-5 (Online)
ISBN: 978-1-80382-561-8 (Epub)

ISOQAR certified
Management System,
awarded to Emerald
for adherence to
Environmental
standard
ISO 14001:2004.

Certificate Number 1985
ISO 14001

INVESTOR IN PEOPLE

CONTENTS

LIST OF FIGURES AND TABLES

Figures

Tables

ABOUT THE AUTHOR

 Vickie Cox Edmondson is an Academic and Management Strategist, known as a Forward Thinking, Business-minded Professor, and Engaging Speaker with more than 20 years of industry experience and business consulting. She served as the first Associate Provost for Student Success at Morehouse College. Her research has been published in the *Academy of Management Learning and Education, Journal of Management Education, Journal of Business Ethics, Business and Society, Journal of Organizational Change Management, Journal of Developmental Entrepreneurship,* etc. She received a BA from Spelman College, an MBA from Mercer University, and a PhD in Strategic Management from the University of Georgia.

FOREWORD

In the foreword to the first edition of *The Thinking Strategist: Unleashing the Power of Strategic Management to Identify, Explore and Solve Problems*, David A. Thomas, the 12th president of Morehouse College, Atlanta, GA, described the need for readers at all levels to have and understand the tools presented by Dr. Vickie Cox Edmondson to be able to think strategically about how to respond to conditions in real time. As a Senior Business Finance major at Morehouse, I had the honor and privilege of sitting on the receiving end of Dr. Cox Edmondson's instruction. Not only did she help my peers and I become strategic thinkers, but, like Morehouse, Dr. Cox Edmondson also held a crown above the heads of her students and challenged us to grow tall enough to wear it. The crown was the crown of drive, the crown of determination, the crown of grit, the crown of thought leadership, the crown of trusted advisor, and the crown of excellence. Consequently, I, like many others of her students at Morehouse and other institutions, have been able to wear a crown to drive results, embrace change, and provide a big picture focus at the decision-making table. Not as a king, but as a collaborative and competent leader and team player.

As I reminisce about sitting in the Bank of America Lecture Hall at Morehouse in 2010, the challenges we faced and solved as students in our capstone business course taught by Dr. Cox Edmondson come to mind. Whether it was determining the root cause for Abercrombie and Fitch's discrimination policies and practices or enhancing Nike's supply chain to make it a more efficient company, we used available resources to face those respective challenges. With Dr. Cox Edmondson's thought-provoking guidance, we developed and justified strategies to not only improve profitability, but chart a path for each company's long-term success. While we had textbooks, articles, magazines, and the Internet at our disposal as tools in our quest to become strategic thinkers, we did not have *The Thinking Strategist* textbook to leverage.

But look no further: you, college students and business professionals alike, have in your hands a roadmap to be a thoughtful and skilled thinking strategist, able to think critically and strategically. Thus, you can enhance your chances of being selected for opportunities and advanced in your career. The global pandemic caused swift changes in business practices and even etiquette. This edition of *The Thinking Strategist* builds on the strategic perspectives evidenced in the first edition and can be used as a textbook or as a reference in professional decision situations. It will help to you develop the critical thinking skills necessary to navigate seas that could be still, turbulent, or experiencing crashing waves. The bonus is the "For Your Toolbox" exercises. I am confident that if you fully examine the challenges, you will cultivate a strategic mindset that will be beneficial for your personal and professional goals.

Reader: *The Thinking Strategist* will stretch you to become the leader you are destined to be. Whether you believe strategizing is in your DNA or you want to learn to be a strategic thinker, please be advised: **this book will not do the work for you.** To achieve what Cox Edmondson refers to as expert status, you must see yourself as the winner you will be in the future, set goals, come up with a plan, execute repeatedly, and learn from missteps. And, depending on where you are in the world today, that plan may evolve and mutate.

Dr. Vickie Cox Edmondson gave my class quite the challenge. Embrace the work irrespective of who (your capstone professor, your boss, your business partner, your mentor) is encouraging you to become a thinking strategist. While attaining that crown was grueling, the content which can be found in The Thinking Strategist was and is still relevant. It has paid dividends over my career in banking.

I am forever grateful.

Jonas Robinson
Director, BMO Capital Markets

ACKNOWLEDGMENTS

In the foreword to the first edition of *The Thinking Strategist*, Morehouse College president and scholar, David A. Thomas, wrote that *The Thinking Strategist* is the first book to address changes in how decision making occurs in what he and some futurists have coined a VUCA world. A world that is volatile, uncertain, complex, and ambiguous. According to Thomas, "It describes the tools of strategy making in an accessible way. Professor Vickie Cox Edmondson makes a compelling case for why being a **thinking strategist** is necessary whether you are a senior manager trying to break through to the next level or a person early in your career."

This revision furthers my commitment to motivate and inspire confidence in individuals from traditionally excluded groups who work in deadline and budget driven roles in high performance and competitive organizational cultures. Much has changed since the first edition appeared in 2018. It can be more difficult to be a person of color working in a predominantly White organization (PWO) given the increased and racial animus and accompanying beliefs toward diversity, equity, and inclusion (DEI). On the other hand, organizations that value the business case for DEI have increased their commitment to DEI in words and deeds. Thus, this new edition seeks to better prepare diverse contributors to make a difference at the decision-making table.

Again, I express my sincere appreciation to my students and faculty colleagues at the University of Georgia, the University of Alabama at Birmingham, Morehouse College, and Tuskegee University. Over the years, they have forced me to make tough decisions and deliver upon my promises. I celebrate their successes and milestones as they reach their career goals. I certainly want to thank the authors who have provided content for my courses over the years.

Lastly, I want to express my appreciation to my core supporters who I can count on in every endeavor to cheer me on and to provide the practical assistance needed for my success, my legacy daughters: Shantori, Devon, and Brandy.

NOTE ON SUPPLEMENTARY MATERIAL

A complete set of PowerPoint slides and a study guide is available to assist adopters in preparing for classroom and business presentations. These learning and teaching aids can be found at www.emerald.com.

PART ONE

SETTING EXPECTATIONS

SECTION A

SEE YOURSELF AT THE TOP

Would you like to be considered one of the most widely sought-after candidates for a position in your company or chosen field, for entrance into top graduate and professional schools in the world, or someone destined to make your mark as an entrepreneur or a leader in causes and movements that matter to you? Are you willing to put in the work to achieve that level of success? Don't waste your time with this book if you are not. Reading it may make you believe you can achieve success if you can recall or refer back to the key points, but you won't know how good you can really be until you believe the advice and tools found within can open doors for you. Once you put in the work, you will be more empowered to achieve your hopes, dreams, and aspirations even if being at the top is not one of your goals.

1

WHAT IS STRATEGY AND WHY IS IT IMPORTANT TO ANYONE NOT AT THE TOP?

In business, products or services are offered for sale or use more often than not by more than one manufacturer, seller, or merchandizer. Competition among firms in an industry can be fierce. The moves and approaches used to entice employees, investors, customers, clients to respond more favorably to your business, and products and services than to the competition are referred to as strategy. The moves and approaches used to position your business for growth are referred to as strategy. The moves and approaches used to respond to threats in the industry are referred to as strategy. Strategy can be defined as a set of decisions, approaches, and actions aimed at successfully meeting financial and strategic objectives over time. Objectives are countless and may vary from year to year and change from leadership team to leadership team (Fig. 1). Many of the decisions are made at the top, therefore you might ask, "Why is strategy important for those who are not at the top?" and "Why should I become an expert at strategy well before I am in position to determine strategy?"

While many of the *final decisions* are made at the top, many *intermediate decisions* are made throughout the organization and well before a set of recommendations are brought to the attention of top management for consideration (Fig. 2). For example, top management may decide which new widgets will be produced in the upcoming year. However, there are many factors about each widget and its capacity to help a company successfully compete against other firms that must be determined well before the new product conceptions are presented to the decision makers – those people in a company that are considered experts and are ultimately responsible for the success of

5

Fig. 1.   Hierarchical Management Structure with Multiple Strategic Business Units.

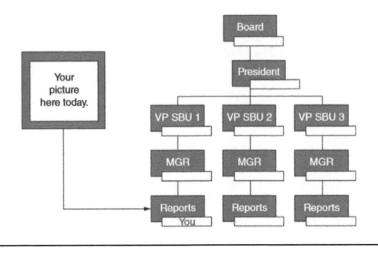

Fig. 2.   Flat Management Structure for a Small Entrepreneurial Venture or Single Business Unit.

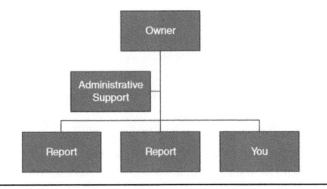

a company. Imagine you are observing a comparative presentation where the decision makers consider which new products, if any, they will support. More than likely, you will observe some of the decision makers ask probing questions that help to determine which product or products to select. Some decision makers will make comments that may adjust the thinking of the presenters as well as the other decision makers. Someone may display an unwillingness to change and must be coached for a change of position.

YOUR PROFESSIONAL GROWTH

While observing strategic decision making in action could be enlightening and quite motivational, waiting until you are in a position to "set" or determine the final strategy is too late to develop distinctive competencies in strategic thinking and decision making. The sooner you begin to use intentional strategies in your work life, the easier it will be to handle the role of setting strategy for a firm once the competencies are needed. As a contributor, you will be judged on your ability to make better decisions and solve problems before they occur. The quality of your input can help you get noticed and considered for promotions sooner than your colleagues. At the core of this book is the goal to help you develop the skills that will allow you to be a skillful decision maker as well as a driver of decision making – an expert, a thinking strategist.

Business coaches Graham Alexander, Alan Fine, and Sir John Whitmore developed the GROW Model in the 1980s as a coaching model. Their model has been adapted over the years (Fine & Merrill, 2010). The adaption below will serve as a guide for your professional development throughout this book:

- Goal setting (what do you personally want to achieve and how does it help the organization).

- Reality (is the goal attainable, what obstacles must you overcome, and how long will it take you to get there).

- Opportunities (what conditions are favorable for you).

- Way forward (what is your success strategy).

As posited by the Department of Health and Human Services (n.d.) (a department of the US government whose aim is to help those who are least able to help themselves), as you gain more opportunities, you are expected to contribute more to the organization and to the proficiency of others in order to facilitate either an action or a decision. Leadership competencies include:

- *Expert*: models, leads, trains, and motivates multiple levels of personnel to be excellent in decisiveness.

- *Advanced*: even in the most difficult situations, recognizes problems or opportunities and determines whether action is needed, takes charge of a group when it is necessary to facilitate a decision, and makes decisions in a timely manner under ambiguous circumstances and when there exists considerable risk.

- *Proficient*: usually recognizes problems or opportunities and determines whether action is needed, takes charge of a group when it is necessary to facilitate a decision, and makes decisions in a timely manner under ambiguous circumstances and when there exists considerable risk.

- *Novice*: demonstrates common knowledge or understanding of being decisive but may avoid or miss opportunities to make decisions in a timely manner. Sometimes it considers consequences and risks to assess the timing for a decision, uses clear criteria for and includes others in the decision making process, and makes decisions in a timely manner when the options and consequences are clear (Fig. 3).

Fig. 3. The Skill–Opportunity Paradox.

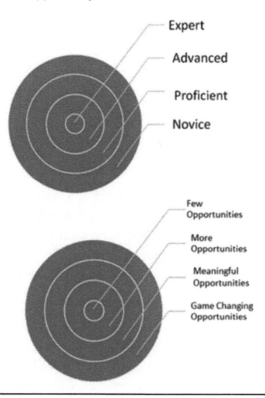

WHAT DOES IT TAKE TO BECOME AN EXPERT IN STRATEGY?

Before we think about what it takes to be an expert, let us consider some of the things it takes to be proficient through the lens of mathematicians Fuson, Kalchman, and Bransford (2005):

- Conceptual understanding: comprehension of concepts and theory of how they relate to one another.

- Skill fluency: skill in carrying out the phases of strategy making flexibly, accurately, efficiently, and appropriately.

- Adaptive reasoning: capacity for rational thought, reflection, explanation, and justification based on data in addition to natural instinct and intuition.

- Productive disposition: inclination to perceive the process as sensible, useful, and worthwhile, coupled with a commitment to learn and grow.

Simply put, two interrelated factors will determine your success:

1. Realistic Expectations of Success

Expectations guide rational thinking. When we look into the long-term success of any organization, there is a positive correlation between its ability to craft and implement appropriate strategies to solve problems and the organization's long-term success. It seems obvious that the strategies developed by organizations have been undertaken with a sincere belief that their successful implementation will improve the situation. In fact, one can easily say that it is illogical and improbable that decision makers might intentionally craft strategies they believe will make the situation worse. It is, therefore, safe to assume that any change is undertaken with the expectation of improving or limiting the negative impact of an issue to positively affect the performance of the organization. While we can agree on the good intentions of decision makers and everyone involved in the strategy making process, a strong look at the results of their actions tends to present another picture–one of less-than-optimal results.

2. Learning from Repeated Practice

Without question, the primary way to develop competency as a thinking strategist is to participate intentionally and actively in the strategy making process. No matter how many articles and books you read, how many case studies you analyze, how many discussions over coffee you have with experts, how many times you watch someone else do something you want to learn to do well, to become an expert you must to do the thing you want to learn, learn from that experience (analyzing what went as expected, what went better than expected, and what did not go as expected) and practice as often as necessary learning from each experience, making necessary adjustments based on the previous experience. With each decision making opportunity, you can integrate the new knowledge and skills as part of your natural style. Moreover, once you become skilled, the expectation is that you will help others succeed in becoming skilled. Thus, a company benefits from having more thinking strategists because of your efforts.

HOW WILL YOU KNOW WHEN YOU HAVE ACHIEVED EXPERT STATUS?

Inherent to expert status is the idea of comparison to others or relevant strength. Articles and books will help you learn the vocabulary and perhaps ensure you know in which context the terminology is used or how the tactic should work. However, as in any competition, until you get into the game you won't know how good you are in comparison to others. While some argue that you should only compare yourself to how far you have come since the last time you evaluated yourself, and thus not compete with others, self-awareness ensures that your assessment places you among others on the decision makers' radar.

Let us go back to the meeting where the decision makers are considering which widgets to produce in the upcoming year. A thinking strategist will pay attention to the presenters' communication style, the content of their presentation, the process they use to present the information, etc. Attention would also be paid to the decision makers' understanding and appreciation of the presentation content, their engagement with the presenters, and their willingness to objectively compare all widgets under consideration. The thinking strategist is pondering which presenters are experts at what they do for the firm and what competencies they have that should be emulated or modeled throughout the firm. There may be some thought as to how some people were selected as decision makers if their contributions are not meaningful.

A signal that you are NOT an expert is when you realize that you do not objectively compare well to those whom *you* have determined to be experts. Certainly, your assessment of the decision makers' competencies may differ from others as your direct knowledge of their knowledge, skills, and contributions to a company may be limited. However, an introspective self-assessment of *your* competencies will reveal areas for improvement that only *you* can confirm or deny.

You will know you are becoming an expert when you are invited to the decision making table as a member of your workgroup or to represent your workgroup. Your work output has shown signs that you are a contributor worthy of closer attention – based on your knowledge of the internal and external environment of business, your attention to detail, creativity, innovation, adaptability (learn new skills), and willingness to change the status quo. When you are at the decision making table, you now have an edge that will allow you to become more proficient and thus more valuable to a company. You will become a go-to resource for others in a company.

Likewise, you will know you are becoming an expert when your network includes key decision makers throughout the organization. Intentionally build your support network by connecting with others with similar goals and interests. Learn what others do in your department and your company. Invest in their success. Connect with colleagues and others in your industry to learn more about different functions that can help you develop your competency to problem solving.

This book seeks to provide business students and aspiring decision makers with an overview of what it takes to be an expert in the strategic management process. Given learners differ in the ways that they perceive and comprehend information, not everyone achieves expert status at the same rate. Many people find the competencies hard to attain, regardless of how often they practice or are invited to the table. Moreover, someone can be an expert in one phase and a novice in another. However, most succeed, to varying degrees. Few people become experts. However, the more expertise you have the more game changing opportunities you are presented. The better you become at setting yourself apart from others for making a difference for others – not just yourself, the more opportunities you get to contribute.

Fig. 4. The Strategic Management Process.

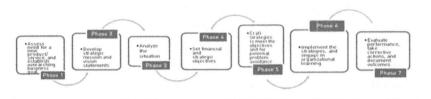

As shown in Fig. 4, there are countless opportunities for you to contribute to the strategy making process. The process will be introduced in Chapter 2 and each phase will be discussed further in Part II. As you move through the process, it will become increasingly clear that it is not a linear step-by-step process and that the amount of time required for each phase differs. Moreover, depending on who is at the table, conducting some processes is more challenging than others are. Nonetheless, each phase is necessary for optimal performance, and you should strive to be more than proficient in each phase to make good contributions. Successful leaders understand that it is the collective strength (the interdependencies of factors, both positive and negative, that determine competitive positioning) of the process and the competencies of the people utilizing the process that determine its success.

A Thinking Strategist's Toolbox

A toolbox can help you develop your thinking process and track how you make success happen so that you can help others. To help you along the way, I included some suggested entries. Don't stop with those. Descriptions of any incident that supports or questions your assumptions and beliefs should be added to the toolbox.

2

THE PROCESS, THE PLAYERS, AND THE STAKES

Before discussing the phases of the strategy making process, Chapter 2 explores the arena in which businesses operate. In particular, I introduce concepts related to ecosystems, industries, and stakeholder management theory. For clarity, the terms *business, company, organization, and firm* are used throughout *The Thinking Strategist*. The term *business* represents an economic system where products (goods) and services are exchanged for money or something of value to the other party and refers to business as a collective institution or trade. In all other cases, as in practice, the terms *company, organization, or firm* are interchangeable and used to identify one entity. Lastly, no distinction is made in this book regarding profit motive unless it is considered necessary to explain a concept.

ECOSYSTEMS

In the last three decades, firms have moved away from a narrow industry perspective to a business ecosystem view. Scholars describe an ecosystem as a collective strategy where stakeholders work cooperatively and competitively to support new products, satisfy customer needs, thus gradually become a structured community (Moore, 1993; Neumeyer, Santos, & Morris, 2019). Edmondson, Zebal, Bhuiyan, Crumbly, and Jackson (2021) set forth a comprehensive ecosystem model that explores the functions that role model actors (existing Black-owned firms, their supply chain, those involved in their unconventional entrepreneurial marketing and financing efforts) and capacity building actors (scholar-practitioners in business schools, researchers, and advocates) play in the success of aspiring and existing Black American entrepreneurs in the United States. The authors acknowledge that the model can also be applied to firms owned by other racioethnic groups. Understanding who the key actors or players are in your career, the roles they play, and their stakes in a business transaction is important to your success.

INDUSTRY

An industry is a set of companies that seek to solve the same problem. The companies in an industry offer similar products and services, compete for resources, and utilize strategies to achieve their goals. They refer to each other and are referred to by other stakeholders as "the competition."

Companies within an industry vary in size, structure, power, organizational knowledge and talents, and therefore internal problems. Everything that happens in an industry affects each company differently. A thinking strategist will look at an industry situation and ask three questions: (1) Does this situation create an issue (opportunity or threat) for our organization? (2) Does it have the potential to create an issue for our organization? (3) If so, what actions can be taken to exploit the opportunity or to prevent the threat from negatively affecting our outcomes?

Likewise, industries differ, and while some knowledge is considered universally applicable, some industries have their own "language" and ways of doing things that each organization collectively and problem solvers individually should understand to fully participate in or contribute to the problem-solving process. Also, it is important for the key decision makers in an organization to know their industry to fully take advantage of the benefits of being in the industry and to address threats that are presented by simply having a presence in an industry. Governments monitor industries and report on factors facing the competition and outcomes; however, these reports are not in real-time and serve primarily as lagging indicators of industry attractiveness. Industry analysts and pundits provide advice that can be used for better real-time decision making.

STAKEHOLDERS AND STAKEHOLDER POWER

In business, a stake represents an interest in outcomes. Those who have a stake are referred to as stakeholders. Stakeholders can affect or are affected by a firm's objectives, strategies, policies, or practices. Internal stakeholders or primary stakeholders are individuals, groups, and organizations that engage in economic transactions with firms such as owners (investors, shareholders), employees (front-line to top management), customers (direct buyers or end-users/consumers), financiers (donors, sponsors, creditors), and business partners (suppliers, complementors). They are directly involved with the operations of the firm. External stakeholders or secondary stakeholders are individuals, groups and organizations that do not engage in direct economic exchanges with the firm but are affected by its strategies and performance. This group includes not only those who have direct financial concern (potential financiers, the other firms offering the same or similar products or services, industry analysts) but also oversight entities (government entities, industry associations, and the media) and concerned citizens (public, the community, social activists).

Part of an effective strategy making process is consideration of how stakeholders are impacted by business decisions and actions and how they might react when an imbalance of power exists. No doubt you have heard the cries of "business is too big" or "business is too powerful." Business power refers to the capacity business has to make things happen – to be an influencer in decisions and outcomes. There is no judgment in this institutional reality, as judgments should be made at the firm level. Moreover, size does not determine business power. Small firms that are poised to exert influence over stakeholders consistently do have tremendous power. Large firms that are poised to exert influence but do not exert it have little power over stakeholders.

Some firms use their power for the good of self and other stakeholders who have less power. Others use it only for good of self for economic gains. Some use it primarily for the good of other stakeholders (non-profits seeking non-economic gains). Think of stakeholders as players. Each has a stake in the firm and the industry. Some have more than one stake. Each has power; some more than others have. Some exert their power; others do not. Some attempt to exert more power than they have.

Malik, Gupte, Edmondson, and Edmondson (2017)[CE1], identified three types of stakeholders along the power spectrum based on available information: (1) the powerful; (2) the average; and (3) the less powerful. The less powerful group was further separated into three types: satisficers, at a disadvantage, and vulnerable:

1. **Powerful stakeholders** are well equipped to make good business decisions over the long term. This group would be the well-informed stakeholders, who research and inform themselves about the system before making business decisions. These stakeholders can directly influence business decisions.

2. **Average stakeholders** are capable of making decisions because they understand the policies and practices that are currently in place based on their stake, along with the benefits and drawbacks. They may research a company's products or services but fail to gain an understanding of the system that makes it possible for the products or services to be delivered to the customer. Most average stakeholders do not attempt to directly influence business decisions.

3. **Less powerful stakeholders** are the least sophisticated and are not informed enough to understand how the decision making process works or how the proposed decisions impact them. Within this group are:

   a. *satisficers* who voluntarily give up their power and are willing to settle for less than the optimal product or service, or relationship to engage;

   b. stakeholders who *are at a disadvantage* because they are negatively impacted as a result of the policies and practices in place; and

   c. *vulnerable* stakeholders who lack the ability to process how best to decide or who do not have enough information to make a sound business decision.

Let us look at the stakes of some of the key players who are likely to be at the table in the strategy making process.

BOARD OF DIRECTORS

You may never sit at the table with "the Board"; however, you may have an opportunity to influence the board's decision making. The board is in place to govern and oversee the management of a firm. Working with top management, those people who are hired by the board to manage the day-to-day activities, the board helps to set the direction of the firm. The Sarbanes-Oxley Act, also known as the Public Company Accounting Reform and Investor Protection Act of 2002, or SOX, was put in place to protect investor interests and hold boards in publicly traded companies accountable. Although this federal law does not apply to privately owned firms, the documentation that is required can be useful in any setting.

Moreover, when boards are highly involved in the strategy making process, the chances increase that stakeholders, both internal and external stakeholders, will attempt to influence board decisions. Some stakeholders go directly to the board or one of its powerful members to influence board decisions and to influence the decisions of top management.

Composition of Board of Directors:

1. Inside – management directors.

2. Outside – non-employees.

Approaches to Board Appointments:

1. Interlock – executive or director at one firm sits on the board of another.

2. Reciprocal interlock – two firms with executives sitting on each other's boards, two firms share the same director.

3. Indirect interlock – two firms have directors who sit on the board of a third firm.

TOP MANAGEMENT

By now, you've ascertained that "see yourself at the top" alludes to top management – those select few who are considered the final decision making team by most employees. They are expected to provide leadership – to convey a direction to relevant persons and guide the organization toward that direction by way of example, instruction, and actual navigation.

In for-profit organizations, top management is often informally referred to as executive or the C-Suite because their titles begin with C's-Chief Executive Officer (same as President in most cases), Chief Financial Officer, Chief Operating Officer, Chief Information Officer, Chief Technology Officer, etc. Their plush offices are usually located at the corporate headquarters and serve as one of many extrinsic rewards for excellence and exceeding performance expectations.

The C-Suite is usually compensated well and receives additional financial compensation when the organization meets or exceeds performance targets. Thus, their stakes in the strategy making process are high. Each officer in top management answers to the Board of Directors individually and collectively. As inferred, only the Board has the ability to override the decisions of the top management team.

MANAGERS

In addition to the decision makers in the C-Suite, depending on the organization's structure, managers have titles such as Vice President, Director, and simply Manager. Managers are those people in an organization who rely on their experience, relevant and often specialized knowledge to plan, lead, organize, and control the activities that are approved by top management. For the record, as in practice, the terms activities, tactics, or components are used interchangeably in *The Thinking Strategist*. These terms are used to identify individual steps or how to put the strategy in action in strategy implementation.

Note that crafting a strategy is quite different from identifying tactics. A change in strategy requires a new set of activities to meet objectives, whereas a change in tactics is merely a change in a few of the activities that are needed to make the current strategy work. Managers are often invited to the table to provide insights about the status of how a strategy is going at any point in time. Again, depending on the organizational structure, the management reporting and decision making authority, chain of command, may be simple or complex. The more levels, the more complex the decision making process can be. Efforts to simplify the process include removing the need for approvals/signatures at each level within the hierarchy and empowering people to make decisions (by sharing information) and believing that they will perform better than expected.

Not only do managers have positional authority to determine how best to implement strategy and are empowered to make intermediate decisions during the process, but they also have a duty to get the work done through others. They have the authority to hire the best candidates, promote those who are capable of handling more responsibilities, and terminate relationships with underperforming stakeholders (i.e., employees and suppliers). They also have the authority to hire and partner with their friends, promote those with whom they like doing business, and terminate relationships with performers they simply don't like. Yet, they too are required to answer to someone regarding their decisions, especially when their judgment and decisions affect the success of a strategy. In all cases, managers are managed by a manager at the next level up in the organizational structure.

EMPOWERED PROBLEM SOLVERS AND CONTRIBUTORS

Employees play a fundamental role in the strategy making process. In an organization of one, this individual is responsible for performing the work. However, in organizations that have hired help additional people contribute to outcomes. Whether the group consists of only the owner, 5, 50, 500, 5,000, 50,000 persons, etc., this group makes things happen on a routine basis.

For the remainder of this text, employees, or workers, regardless of title, will be thought of as empowered problem solvers and contributors and referred to simply as problem solvers and contributors. Let us assume that everyone employed by an organization has good intentions, is competent to perform position duties, wants to contribute to the success of organizations regardless of position power or authority, and that managers have empowered them to use their strengths to make an impact. In cases where there is a misfit between job duties and the individual, this situation is an opportunity for a human resource professional to develop and implement a strategy for employee development or job redesign. The act of referring to employees or workers as problem solvers and contributors fundamentally removes the stigma that someone, particularly those who do not hold a management position – those on the front-line, feels like he or she is "just an employee."

As a stakeholder group, these individuals have responsibilities that are assumed necessary to solve the problem/achieve the overarching organizational goal that determines why an organization exists. Their outcomes determine the success of a strategy, and ultimately the success of a firm. Thus, their competence should be continually developed to eliminate signs of incompetence during implementation.

Thinking strategists, regardless of their level of responsibility, will assess how their role helps to achieve the overarching organizational goal, vision, mission, and objectives of the company and find ways to ensure that role is seen as contributing to firm success. In my role as the Associate Provost for Student Success at Morehouse College, I was responsible for developing and overseeing a strategic management process to retain and graduate more than 2,100 students, most of whom are Black males, pursuing a BA or BS degree within three academic divisions. One of the four areas I supervised was the Academic Success Center, formerly the Learning Resource Center. Prior to my appointment, the Center had served as a place to study for students with limited offerings, primarily a computer lab and a place for students to print. Clearly, there was room for enhancing how the Center staff served both students and faculty. I appointed a new Center Director and empowered her to bring a new vision to life based on years of experience in student development. Moreover, I helped to brand the Center as a true academic resource for students including converting space to a resource room and converting unused rooms into offices so that the Center could house advising and student support staff. Another unused space was converted to serve as the office for the Coordinator of Academic Advising and Faculty Support, a job redesign that I put into effect so that a professional advisor could provide guidance on best practices to faculty advisors. Moreover, I also personally financed four modern Scandinavian armless chairs to create a reading nook for Center guests. The changes that were made were not radical and did not require enormous funds. They merely required a team of empowered problem solvers to work diligently together with a shared goal – helping students do well academically.

OTHER STAKEHOLDERS

The other internal stakeholders in the strategy making process may not be sitting at the decision making table; however, their interests in economic transactions are the heart of discussions. Owners (investors, shareholders) expect a financial return on their investment, customers (direct buyers or end-users/consumers) expect products and services that will meet their needs, business partners (suppliers, complementors) expect the firm to be able to deliver on its promises, and financiers (donors, sponsors, creditors) want to know the firm is behaving responsibly with money and resources appropriated for business use. Their expectations are legitimate based on contractual and informal relationships. As such, they should be considered influencers whose stakes are also high.

Those players sitting at the table are required to determine how to balance conflicting demands among stakeholders, including the aforementioned external stakeholders that do not engage in direct economic exchanges with the firm. A conflict is a dilemma between two or more demands or actions. Prior to making decisions or solving problems, a thinking strategist seeks to understand the needs and possible demands of each stakeholder and how those demands interact with other stakeholders and with the firm. Contemplate how stakeholders with shared interests can help the firm achieve its goals and become trusted allies that will cooperate (play an active role as needed). Focus on the development and maintenance of quality relationships with stakeholders for mutual benefit and try not to engage in high-cost relationships which demand more time, money, and effort than deemed reasonable, simply because there appears to be a lack of suitable stakeholders willing to cooperate. The goal with managing stakeholders is a win-win-win situation in which the firm wins – the individual stakeholder wins – and the collective group of stakeholders wins.

Building rapport with stakeholders over time increases the chances of having a relationship that you can have confidence in and, therefore better predict outcomes. Factors that indicate a mutually beneficial relationship exists:

- a balance of power relative to what each player puts into the relationship and what they get out of it;

- a willingness of each player to be vulnerable to the actions of the other player with an expectation that the other player is dependable and can be relied on to deliver on its promises;

- a willingness to cooperate or at least cause no harm to each other's interests; and

- an expectation that when a stakeholder "calls-in" a favor, the request will be reasonable.

Confidence is defined as the perception that another party has the ability to perform as expected. Do not confuse confidence with trust. You can have confidence in another party but not trust them. For example, vulnerable consumers may turn to shady car dealers at pay-here lots in their quest to purchase an inexpensive used car because they or others they know have been turned down by lenders at traditional banks due to their credit score. They may not trust the lenders at the pay-here dealership to give them the lowest rates, but they have confidence that they will help them achieve their goals. More on vulnerable stakeholders will be in Chapter 3.

THE PROCESS

The strategy making process is formally referred to as the strategic management process. In any process, related activities are grouped together as one phase. As shown in Fig. 4 (p. 12), the process has seven distinct phases. In Phase 1, a problem that needs to be resolved is assessed to determine if a new product or service is needed. Other companies may have attempted to resolve the problem, but the person(s) who conducted this assessment may see missed opportunities that can be pursued. If the assessment shows promise, then an overarching business goal to address that need/problem is established. In Phase 2, mission statements and vision statements are developed to provide direction for the decisions that will drive the firm now and in the future. In Phase 3, research is conducted to determine if industry conditions are suitable for the desired mission and vision. If the demand exists and the company can handle the demand or has commitments from strategic partners to collaborate to meet the demand, then the process continues. In Phase 4, financial and strategic objectives are set. In Phase 5, strategies to meet those objectives and to address potential problems that may arise during implementation are crafted. In Phase 6, the strategies are implemented and problems and opportunities that actually arise are noted. In Phase 7, performance is evaluated, and corrective actions are taken to ensure that what is learned is documented and can be applied in the future. Each phase will be detailed in later chapters of this book.

The process is not a phase-by-phase process, but it is a dynamic process in which a phase can be revisited, skipped, out of order. Moreover, some terms are interchangeable. For example, deciding which strategy to use, formulating strategy and crafting strategy represent one distinct phase in the process. In Fig. 4, this activity is Phase 5. The only way that you would know that these three activities are the same is if you understand what Phase 5 of the process involves. Moreover, if you were told by a colleague there were only four phases in the process and you listened closely, you should be able to ascertain if Phase 5 is labeled differently or if Phase 5 has been left out entirely.

The process is only a means to success. Success is the goal. As a result of this process, we should see an improvement in decision making and outcomes. Thinking strategists cannot be reluctant to adjust their thinking, adjust what has been decided, or admit that something needs additional attention.

GETTING ALL BRAINS ON DECK

Players rarely work alone. Some degree of teamwork and collaboration is needed to achieve organizational goals and meet objectives. Employment and, subsequently, an appointment to a board, team, or task force signal that a person has demonstrated he or she has knowledge and competencies valued by an organization. The best way to demonstrate your value is to do well as a trusted, intuitive, and competent team player. Fig. 5 depicts interactions among common roles that are evident in teams:

1. a facilitator;

2. a leader;

3. contributors;

4. participators; and

5. free riders.

Three interactions needed to maximize the collective intelligence to ensure a team is productive are facilitation, leadership, and contribution. While it is common for team members to work alone and then combine their work at the end, this practice disadvantages the team. Teams that work collectively have a better chance of meeting their objectives. For optimal success, team

Fig. 5.   Common Team Roles.

members have to trust each other and believe that other members are capable and willing to perform as agreed and required for success. Robbin Starks O'Neal, the Shipping and Receiving Supervisor at OFS Optics in Carrollton, GA, a global fiber options designer and manufacturer, captured the essence of teamwork and collaboration as:

> *I will not ask you to do anything that I won't do for you. I will not ask you to do something that benefits US that I am not willing to do or have not already done… We are in it together. We win as a team. We need each other doing his or her part(s) for the best results.*

Facilitation is needed to ensure that the team understands the strategy process that will be used, that the process is followed, and that the process is adapted when it does not produce desired outcomes early on. As a facilitator, it is important to communicate often and effectively to ensure that other contributors know their roles and expectations. It is also important that if a facilitator has duties on a project, he or she completes the work in an exemplary way (e.g., meet or exceed deadlines, display a can-do inspiring attitude).

Leading or leadership is needed to ensure that the team understands the strategy content that is needed to inform, educate, and provide insights that will ultimately help the decision makers accept the work that will be presented to them. Although someone on the team may hold the title of team leader, leadership is expected from every member. No person's ideas should be accepted as sacrosanct, no questions asked; but those who have knowledge on a subject matter have a responsibility to provide their insights and help lead the team in an informed direction.

While effective facilitation and leadership can help a team meet its objectives, contribution from every member on the team is needed to ensure that each team member provides his/her unique perspectives, experiences, and resources that will add value to the team. Contributing to a team is different from participating on a team. Members contribute when their individual efforts add value to the team's effort. Without it, the team must rely on outcomes from people doing just enough to get the work done (i.e., participation), which may not have the value-add expected by the decision makers and the other members of the team. For example, participants attend meetings, but contributors add the voices needed to aid in meeting the team's objectives. Failure to participate (i.e., freeriding) can lead to frustration for the rest of team members and if it is noticeable, it will lead to termination. On the other hand, when you are known as someone who can be relied on in a team setting, you will be invited to the table again and again.

WHAT CONSTITUTES A GOOD CONTRIBUTION?

It depends. How does the contribution you seek to make tie into the overarching organizational goal or to a particular objective that has been set? Most people are not interested in learning or doing more of the same. How well do you understand how and why something is or is not happening? How well can you explain your understanding and purpose in improving the situation? How confident are you that what you know matters or what you can do will be beneficial to the company? How willing are you to be involved in the process to make a difference? How do you handle free riders who give the appearance of participating but are not? Considering these questions and making necessary adjustments before contributing is necessary to avoid the appearance that your information/skill is not worthy of further consideration in the decision making process. Too many moments of low influence can lead to you no longer receiving an invite to the table. More about managing contributions can be found in Part II, Chapter 9.

Decision makers rely on everyone at the table to contribute good information and demonstrate skills that will result in improved organizational performance and lead to a competitive advantage in the industry. Your immediate mission is to get to the table and stay there.

For Your Toolbox

Here's an opportunity for you to think about the people invited to the table or getting opportunities around you? Write down what you admire about them. What characteristic do they portray that would make you conclude they are a thinking strategist or are they just lucky? What skills have they obtained that sets them apart? How do you compare?

3

THE ART OF JUDGMENT

Just because a company can do things, does not mean it should. Archie Carroll (1979) noted that businesses have a corporate social responsibility to behave in a way that is economically profitable, complies with the law, is ethical, and upholds the social contract between business and society. As pointed out by philosopher Howard Thurman, a corporation may not have a conscience, but those in leadership positions must take responsibility for the decisions they make, and the lives affected by those decisions, and not shift responsibility or blame to others (Thurman, 1998, p. 161). Yet for decades, strategies have been implemented to retain key stakeholders at any cost, with little regard for whether those strategies left them less well-off. Although the board and top management set aspirational values or the standards for ethical decision making, the ability to make sound judgments or to form an opinion and come to a conclusion about a phenomenon under consideration is a job expectation or duty of everyone in the strategic management process. However, contributors are often forced to find trade-offs that they and the organization's stakeholders can "live with" or accept.

Ethics is defined as going beyond what the law requires in decision situations. Decision makers have a responsibility to know the laws and regulations that affect them and their work, and to know the consequences when they and others fail to abide by the rules. Consider, in Chapter 2, we explored both business and stakeholder power. Carroll and coauthor Ann Buchholtz (2006) assert that power cannot be viewed in isolation from responsibility.

They discussed personal and organizational ethics. Whereas they note that personal ethics surfaces in situations outside the work context, organizational ethics are the set of personal ethics found within the work context.

There is an assumption that people want to behave ethically in both situations. When it comes to business ethics, Carroll and Buchholtz assert that individuals face ethical quandaries on a daily basis but often have no background or training in business ethics or ethical decision making to help them decide what can and should be done. You may find yourself sitting at the table with individuals who have different ethics or work values than yours. You may find yourself right in the middle of something that you perceive to be unethical decision making. A mismatch between company expectations and an individual's judgment of how a company should address the needs of its stakeholders can lead to increased stress, job dissatisfaction, and concerns about long-term job security. This situation leads to loss of good talent.

INDIVIDUAL PURPOSE AT WORK

Perhaps you have heard people say that not everyone is "cut out" to work in an industry or at a particular company within the industry. Implied in this sentiment is that some behaviors are more suitable to some industries than others are. You have an identity apart from your title and place of work. You determine how closely your personal identity and work identity align. The closer they align, the more you can be your authentic self at work. Thus, soul searching is a key component in the strategic management process. Two questions are often considered: What does success look like in this firm and industry? and What am I willing to do to be successful? Over time, ethical conclusions of the collective persons making decisions become the company's identity within the industry, and there will be a perception that you share that identity (Cox, 1991).

While examining a company's code of ethics, and mission and vision statements can help determine if a company is a good fit for career opportunities, determining whether their daily work provides someone with a sense of purpose has become more salient in decision making. Life events such as COVID-19 and movements like Black Lives Matter cause people to reflect on their purpose in life and to consider the kind of work they do. As noted by partners at McKinsey & Co. (Dhingra, Samo, Schaninger, & Schrimper, 2021), contributors expect their jobs to bring a significant sense of purpose to their lives. When there is a disconnect between what the company expects of its people and an individual's perception of what he or she should do in a role, there is a greater likelihood that the individual is feeling unfulfilled with the work and is likely to look for other opportunities or leave the organization.

Given the pressures of the strategy making process, it is not surprising that teams have conflict. Putting personal or functional self-interest over team outcomes is a real source of conflict. Moreover, in a company culture that embraces honest feedback to improve job performance, notably where contributors are more task-oriented than people-oriented, an unwillingness to speak up about poor performance or unacceptable behavior of your colleagues means that you are part of the problem. Remember that you don't need to be friends with colleagues, clients, or classmates, but you do need to have a productive relationship that can tolerate feedback.

EMOTIONAL INTELLIGENCE AND ASSESSMENT TOOLS

An important part of exercising the art of judgment as a thinking strategist is having the emotional intelligence to handle the pressures that come with being in a decision making role. Again, will you always agree with your colleagues or the decision makers about which strategy works best? No, it is highly unlikely. Emotional intelligence reflects your ability to control your emotions and to respond to the emotions of others in the moment to bring about collaboration and productivity. Perhaps you have observed some really smart and capable people who are easily frustrated, cannot handle bad news, or cannot work well under extreme pressure. Or you have observed some people who are really good at what they do and are go-getters, but they are seen as overly aggressive and unable to empathize with their colleagues in real time. The first scenario represents underdone strengths or not using your strengths when necessary to be successful. The second scenario represents overdone strengths or using the strength to the degree that it becomes a weakness. Overdone and underdone strengths can trigger interpersonal conflicts and harm working relationships, especially when both parties involved lack emotional intelligence.

In the decision making process, problem solvers must ask tough questions and challenge conventional thinking. Emotional intelligence is a sign of maturity that reflects an ability to learn new things and to unlearn what you thought to be true. In doing so, individuals show a willingness to respond to situations with the objective in mind rather than respond based on their personal feelings about what is happening or who is leading the charge. Developing this skill can help move you from an average (proficient) performer to a high (advanced) performer. Of course, it hurts to receive negative feedback. However, thinking strategists view feedback as an opportunity to get better at what they do or to get better at explaining their views or messaging.

DEVELOPING EMOTIONAL INTELLIGENCE

Human resource development professionals conduct assessments to assist organizations in determining individual success potential, to explore whether a person is a good fit for the organization, and to help individuals improve their productivity based on personality, preferences, and behaviors. In addition to emotional quotient assessments that seek to determine if individuals have the emotional intelligence that is needed to make key decisions; common assessment tools are:

1) Myers-Briggs Type Indicator identifies one of 16 types based on preferences.

2) DISC Profile identifies a blend of four behavior and personality styles.

3) StrengthsFinder identifies your top five strengths out of a possible 34 deemed necessary to work with others. However, it does not address your top five weaknesses.

4) Self-Deployment Inventory (SDI) identifies one of seven motivational values and one of 13 conflict sequences that impact relationships and job performance.

In 1970, Philosopher Bertocci, claims Carter (2006), defined personality as something that is:

> learned as a person interacts with other persons; more exactly, a person's personality is his more or less systematic mode of response to himself, to others, and to his total environment in the light of what he believes them to be, and what they actually are. (p. 95)

Often a gap exists between how people perceive themselves and how they actually respond in situations. Thus, these tools require an expert to interpret the results and translate them into effective action. The results of the assessments provide the basis for executive coaching that can serve as an intervention to help those who lack the emotional intelligence required to handle the decision making process and improve their ability to engage. If your company does not provide these assessments or you can't afford executive coaching, perhaps you can identify a trusted mentor who can offer advice, a listening ear, and direct you to additional free resources.

Additionally, if your company offers an Employee Assistance Program (EAP), avail yourself of this benefit to get help not only with work-related problems or organizational challenges, but also with personal issues that may be negatively impacting your job performance. EAP services are usually outsourced and have strict confidentiality rules about treatment. Although the EAP service will provide a general report to HR with totals of services provided and types of problems addressed, names are not included. However, if you are referred to EAP for disciplinary problems by your manager or supervisor, you will be required to sign a release (of information) in order for the EAP servicer to provide the organization with limited feedback about your individual's attendance, compliance, and outcomes.

DEVELOPING BETTER JUDGMENT

Once gaps or needs to improve judgment have been disclosed, the thinking strategist should take personal responsibility to address the issues that will close the gap. One-on-one executive coaching and attending workshops and continuing education courses for leadership training can be costly but are well worth the investment. Moreover, countless self-help books are available. Below are five strategies to improve your judgment:

1. Do the research necessary to ensure you have enough information to make an enlightened decision that considers the impact on all stakeholders including you. Be willing to acknowledge that something may not be in your best interest but is in the best interests of the organization.

2. Compare and contrast your opinions to those of your mentor or someone who you respect.

3. Develop your cultural sensitivity to understand and fully consider the views of others from different cultural backgrounds.

4. Own your mistakes and find out where you went wrong and why. Learn to be diplomatic and be not defensive which only exacerbates the issue.

5. Learn from the experience and do not make the same logical mistake twice. When you make judgments note why they were considered as sound or unsound by other contributors and the decision makers.

THE IMPORTANCE OF RESEARCH

A key component of thinking strategically is conducting research. Research is needed regardless of how familiar you are with a topic given how things change in a business environment. Basic steps in a research process are:

Step 1: Do a preliminary search for information through your company's documents, website, emails, etc., to determine the company's stated position or objectives on a topic.

Step 2: Locate additional material/views on the subject in numerous outlets.

Step 3: Evaluate your sources (the outlets and the author's/expert's credentials).

Step 4: Make notes and compare and contrast with your or your company's stated position or objectives, if any.

Step 5: Share your notes/research findings with others on the team. Look for similarities and differences of perspectives from team members. Be willing to change positions.

Step 6: Use the research findings to make recommendations for or against a proposed strategy or tactic. Again, be willing to change positions.

Step 7: File your research for future use should this topic resurface. It can also be used to justify the need to support or change strategies going forward.

DISSENT IN DECISION MAKING

Decision makers are obliged to be open to bad news, dissent, warnings, and problem signs; however, problem solvers and contributors are often afraid to speak up when they disagree or have a divergent view about what is proposed. Let us assume that no one speaks up simply to be considered a troublemaker or naysayer; instead, they offer their objective feedback to avoid groupthink and to offer consideration of another perspective.

An organization's culture determines how most stakeholders respond to what they see going on in an organization. Edmondson and Munchus (2007) presented a model for organizational dissent strategy used during decision making. The model is based on two moderating factors: trust in decision makers and a sense of urgency. As a result, four dissent strategies are identified:

1) *Organizational Communication* – disclosing concerns with those in the organization who can affect the change (trust is high and an urgent need to voice dissent exists.

2) *Organizational Blasting* – disclosing concerns about the unwillingness to act of those in the organization who can affect the change (trust is low and an urgent need to voice dissent exists).

3) *Organizational Rumbling* – disclosing concerns with those in the organization who are unable to effect the change (trust is low and no urgent need to voice dissent exists).

4) *Organizational Silence* – not disclosing concerns to anyone in the organization (when trust is high and no urgent need to voice dissent exists).

The aim is to have everyone communicating with each other at the table when decisions are made (Fig. 6). Blasting, rumbling, and silence are signs of additional problems within the organization's culture that reflect an imbalance of power that must be addressed for informed decision making. Be mindful that although organizational silence is shown to exist when trust is high, it can also exist when trust is low if there is a fear of speaking up. Dissent or opposition to ideas is a healthy part of organizational life. However, conflict is unproductive and leads to ongoing problems if left unresolved. Organizational leaders must be willing to change. In some cases, they may require executive coaching.

Fig. 6.   Edmondson and Munchus Dissent Strategies Model.

ACCOUNTABILITY TO DO SOMETHING

Conducting assessments yields little if the company does little or nothing with the results. Rubina Malik (2015) developed a relationship-based, context-specific informal learning model where information captured from assessments is woven into the decision making process. According to Malik, once something found in the data triggers a need for change in how decisions are made, that trigger or data becomes a consideration throughout the strategic management process. She refers to this increased attention and corrective feedback as the need to "turn up the volume" for improved collaboration and productivity (Fig. 7). The process begins by building trust so that learning can happen, and then establishing a foundation that change is necessary to meet the objective, and ensuring that the kind of feedback

Fig. 7.   Malik Coaching Model.

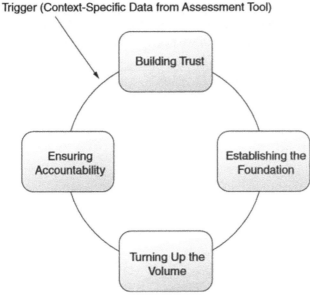

Trigger (Context-Specific Data from Assessment Tool)

Building Trust

Ensuring
Accountability

Establishing the
Foundation

Turning Up the
Volume

needed is available and thus decision makers can be held accountable for their actions.

The key to both the Edmondson and Munchus (2007) model and the Malik (2015) model is building a culture of trust so that, when needed, stakeholders are willing to prompt decision makers to do things differently or to reconsider and perhaps reverse earlier decisions that may lead to poor performance or diminished reputation. Instead, cultures can be developed that encourage ethical decision making and demonstrate care for stakeholders beyond profits.

When top management and the board look back at their strategies and what they accomplished, they should be able to say they were guided by and followed core values that express a duty of care for others. The decisions that are made determine how others view the company and whether a company is worthy of engagement. Stakeholders won't wholeheartedly engage or follow people who purport to espouse values but don't live by them.

For Your Toolbox

Write down some behaviors that would cross the line for you. Note why and how you would respond if any of these behaviors appear to be the only way you can be successful. Describe your final straw – the thing that would lead you to leave the situation (department, company, industry)? Describe what steps you would take to redirect the thinking that put you in this situation.

SECTION B

BUSINESS ACUMEN

A business process consists of structured activities or tasks undertaken to accomplish an outcome. This section is intended to help you articulate standard words, concepts, theories, and methods that are commonly discussed in business. When collaboration is the goal, a common language helps to ensure clarity of thought and intentions, and builds trust and accountability, especially when discussing tough issues. Business graduates and thinking strategists throughout an organization are expected to understand them and be able to apply them when appropriate. Throughout the *The Thinking Strategist*, you will find business concepts that have shared meanings and words that can be used interchangeably (e.g., component/tactic/activity). When presented this way in this book, only one of the terms is necessary in practice. Thinking strategists should choose one and use it consistently for clarity. In many cases, an organization has a preferred way of describing organizational phenomena that you should learn and apply.

Depending on your needs, you might want to skip around in the book. Most people tend to learn best when they need to know something, so skipping around to the things you do not know or that need your immediate attention may be the best use of the book and your time. Some topics require prior knowledge of other topics, so if you're new to strategy, you may find it best to work through the chapters carefully and in order.

4

PROBLEM NOT CURRENTLY SOLVED

Problems are the lifeline to business prosperity and to participation in economic systems. William F. Pounds (1969) noted that a problem could simply be defined as a difference between an actual state and an expected, or often, a desired state. He noted that problems do not have to represent a negative condition but represent the existence of a discrepancy and the discrepancy requires attention and response, even if that response is no action at all.

Similarly, Larry Cochran (1997) defined a problem as a gap between what is and what ought to be. He identified three basic requirements for a problem:

1) a person [stakeholder] must be able to imagine possibilities; what is not present and actual;

2) the gap between what the ideal and the actual must matter to the person [stakeholder]; and

3) the person [stakeholder] is uncertain of how to bridge the gap.

Companies are started to solve problems that are not currently solved. Maybe the problem is solved to some degree or solved in one place but not somewhere else. Maybe the problem exists for a select group. Maybe the problem impacts different groups to varying degrees. Maybe the problem can be solved in a new way. As long as there are identifiable stakeholders who are impacted by a problem that has not been solved, there is a need for an industry to exist. While business can address many problems, there are some problems that are beyond its control and therefore cannot be solved by any company. The role of business in these cases is simply to provide a solution to the part of the problem that can be fixed (Fig. 4).

Driving the process to identify unsolved problems are three central questions: (1) *What problem are we solving?* (2) *What is our business?* and (3) *If we fix this problem, what will our business be in the future?* A company has the potential to succeed as long as (a) the problem exists somewhere for someone and (b) the individuals and entities that the firm relies on to satisfy the needs and wants of those who need the problem solved make the right moves. In most cases, one wrong move will not derail success or cause a company to cease operations. However, the *right* wrong move can create new problems for the company that should not be ignored.

The thinking strategist views a problem as an ability that, left unattended, can impact the capacity of a firm to engage in economic and non-economic exchanges in an optimal way. Rather than saying the firm cannot do something that is under consideration, a thinking strategist looks for ways to make it happen.

BUSINESS MISSION

Phase 2 of the strategy making process involves developing the firm's mission and vision. Once you have determined an answer to the question of "What problem are we solving?" the next pertinent question is "What is our business?" The need to answer this question is twofold:

1) to communicate a common message of why the firm exists to problem solvers and contributors; and

2) to describe the nature of the firm and their business activities to outsiders.

Ensuring that the individuals who are hired by the firm or parties who are interested in partnering with the firm have a clear idea and good understanding of the products or services offered by the firm is essential to the success of the firm.

The mission should be shared in a written mission statement that is not too long or complex. The most effective ones are short, easy to memorize, and memorable to all stakeholders. It should not include the problem or the strategy details. By not including a problem or strategy in the statement, the company has created a situation whereby the stakeholders determine what problem(s) the company is solving based on their interest. Sometimes, unintentionally, or unbeknownst to the firm, an untargeted customer has a place to purchase products or services needed, or a supplier has a place to distribute products. For instance, a company can define itself as a pizza place in its mission statement, which in some stakeholder eyes is quite different from the restaurant. Presumably, a restaurant can serve pizza, but it is not conceptually restricted to do so, and thus it gives the perception that it is skilled in preparing all menu items. While pizza may be the mainstay of the restaurant, a restaurant supplier sees more opportunities for cooperation than if the firm was narrowly defined as a pizza place. In a broader sense, firms can restrict or invite stakeholders to the table through a clear and effective mission statement.

Some companies fail to commit to developing and revising their mission statements when the statement no longer explains what the firm does. Oftentimes, rather than going through the process of changing the statement which may require board approval, companies use catchy slogans. However, slogans don't reveal what the firm does. Instead, slogans are purposed to draw attention to the firm and at best tie the slogan to the firm. For example, a mission statement for a restaurant in an area where busy parents want good food fast might be "Tori's Southern Kitchen serves home-style cooking fast for breakfast and lunch in Atlanta." A slogan such as "Not just good; perfect" is enticing, but it does not provide the insights that stakeholders need to make an informed decision.

STRATEGIC VISION

A strategic vision answers the question: "If we 'fix this problem,' what will our business be in the future?" It has a twofold purpose:

1) identify the business activities the firm intends to pursue; and

2) set forth a long-term direction – a path for developing the firm.

Inherent in this perspective of a strategic vision is that the firm can make progress in solving the problem. A vision statement should be inspiring and motivate problem solvers and contributors to meet and exceed financial and strategic objectives. When stakeholders know what is coming they begin to figure out ways to help bring the vision to fruition. Thinking strategists develop the attitudes, abilities, and skills to be difference makers in the current environment and the one that is on the horizon.

Let us go back to the mission statement: "Tori's Southern Kitchen serves home-style cooking fast for breakfast and lunch in Atlanta." The mission of this restaurant can be changed in three primary ways:

1) change business type [from service to manufacturer (package their best sellers and offer goods for sale in their restaurants) or to merchandizer (purchase inventory and sell it to their customers);

2) increase product offerings/services (breakfast, lunch, and dinner); and

3) increase customer base (throughout the region).

The vision statement could be: "Tori's Southern Kitchen will serve fresh home-style cooking fast for breakfast, lunch, and dinner and offer select packaged goods in the greater Atlanta area." Notice that the vision statement is not vague. It informs the stakeholders of what business the company sees itself doing in the future. The vision statement sets realistic expectations of what is attainable and does not use superlatives such as "the best" or "the grandest" restaurant. Moreover, adding superlatives suggests that the company is not currently the best or the grandest. This may or may not be true, but why attract unnecessary comparisons that are subjective and cannot easily be measured?

As shown in Table 1, the difference between a mission statement and a vision statement is verb tense. A mission statement is always written in the present tense and a vision statement is always written in the future tense. When (the year) mission ends and the vision will be realized is not included in the statements as time is a part of objective setting.

The mission and vision statements tell the world what the company does and plans to do in the future. They help stakeholders make decisions.

Table 1.   Mission and Vision Statement Present Versus Future Tense.

Mission	Vision
We are	We will
	We will be
	We will become

STRATEGIC THINKING TO ANALYZE THE SITUATION

Phase 3 of the strategy making process involves conducting research with the purpose of analyzing the situation to determine what is going on internally and externally prior to making decisions about how to move forward. The strategy making process is not needed for incremental or routine changes; those changes can be handled by writing a policy or codifying a practice to make it a policy. Hickson, Butler, Cray, Mallory, and Wilson (1986) identified three characteristics of strategic decisions:

1) *Rare*: unusual and typically have no precedent to follow.

2) *Consequential*: substantial resources are committed, and a great deal of commitment is demanded from people at all levels.

3) *Directive*: precedents for lesser decisions and future actions are set throughout the organization.

Moreover, when an organization is going through a transformational or structural change, which often involves dealing with high levels of uncertainty and ambiguity, strategic thinking, as a team, to understand the reasons and factors that make that change necessary helps the decision makers make better strategic decisions. As a thinking strategist and a valuable contributor, you can help to remove some of the ambiguity that comes with strategic decision making by using strategic thinking to fill in the details that can be the difference in whether a strategy is considered viable.

Consider strategic thinking as a combination of strategy and critical thinking. Critical thinking is a reflective questioning process used to determine what is happening and what needs to change and how. In the case of strategy making, strategic thinking aims to determine how things can be done differently- better to prepare the organization for the future. Strategic thinking is the generation of ideas and business insights about what to change to gain and leverage a competitive advantage.

CRITICAL VOICING

The Edmondson and Edmondson Critical Voicing Model (2017), as cited in Edmondson and Shannon (2020), depicts how knowledge workers with little formal institutional power influence the larger agenda/strategy based on tacit knowledge not held by others with more formal institutional power. The model assumes that individuals have mastered job-related competencies. In particular, Edmondson and Shannon argue that an ability to weed through data and information is essential when an event or incident triggers the need to pay attention to something that is happening. These events are protective triggers that cause a process to begin, end, or may redirect a process to a different path.

Mobilizing a group of two or more individuals toward a change requires leadership and that capacity exists within each of us. The question is when you are needed, will you choose to lead, or will you sit idly by and do little or nothing? Fig. 8 reveals five critical communication questions Edmondson and Edmondson (2017) identified that drive strategic thinking:

1. What is happening? (critical questioning)

2. Why is this happening? (critical thinking)

3. How does the text portray what is happening? (critical reading)

4. Who has the power to change what is happening? (critical understanding)

5. When will I speak up and do something about what is happening? (critical voicing)

Fig. 8. Edmondson and Edmondson Critical Voicing Model.

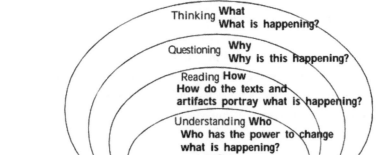

Lastly, thinking strategists have a strategic mindset in which they think strategically about most matters. They constantly think about strategies to resolve issues and the minor details that can derail a strategy. Everyone can develop a strategic mindset. For some, this ability comes naturally. If not, then by applying the information in this book you can become more detail-oriented, a better strategic thinker.

For Your Toolbox

Think about where you work or the field you would like to enter. What problems are you solving? Describe the technical knowledge and skills required in your industry or field. What is your role and what are the expectations of someone in your role? How can you expand your role for better pay and other rewards you seek? Are you willing to help someone who does not have a good understanding of assigned tasks? How might doing so help you in your role?

Write a plan to create an ecosystem to support your aspirations.

5

LEADERSHIP AND DEALING
WITH CHANGE

In Phases 4 and 5 of the strategy management process, decision makers must agree on what they want to accomplish – what they want to change based on the results of the analyses conducted in Phase 3. Before delving into crafting strategy, let us discuss change.

CHANGE AND INNOVATION: WILLINGNESS
TO ACT ON THOUGHTS

In today's competitive environment, we seek not only change but also innovation. Innovation can be disruptive. Hence, change for the sake of change is not wise; it is frustrating especially in organizations that are not built to embrace change. Change requires four things:

1) an acknowledgment that change is needed;

2) a willingness to change;

3) the ability to change; and

4) action.

Eliyahu Goldratt (Goldratt, 1990) expressed the importance of change as a driver in the strategy making process. In explaining the Theory of Constraints (TOC) approach to decision making, as shown in Fig. 9, he set forth three key questions that TOC can help answer:

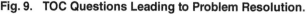

Fig. 9.   TOC Questions Leading to Problem Resolution.

• What to change?	• What to change to?	• How to change?
Problem	Solution	Strategy

1) What to change?

2) What to change to?

3) How to change?

Goldratt (1994) and Goldratt and Cox (1984) noted that every situation has a constraint that needs to be alleviated. Moreover, givens or predetermined boundaries can be imposed on the decision making process. It is good to know your constraints before the analysis begins. Such constraints often include limitations on time, money, people, the scope of what can be done, etc. Regardless of the givens, other constraints are often revealed as the strategy making process ensues.

William Altier (1999) also expressed the importance of analyzing change and argued that given the enormous amount of information in job environs, managers *should only be concerned with information about change.* He goes on to explain two kinds of change and further separates each into two types as depicted in Fig. 10.

Of the four types of change Altier introduced, he argues that planned past change (change that went according to plan) is the only one that does not need to be analyzed given it depicts a situation that happens as planned/ expected and no change is needed. I am in complete agreement with Altier's argument that managers should only be concerned with information about change. However, I disagree that managers should not be concerned with past planned change. At the heart of strategy is the notion, "If it ain't broke, fix it anyway!" After celebrating the success of any strategy, a debriefing of what went right and why is just as important as what went wrong and why. This is particularly important for consistency and

Fig. 10. Adaptation of Altier Change Model #3.

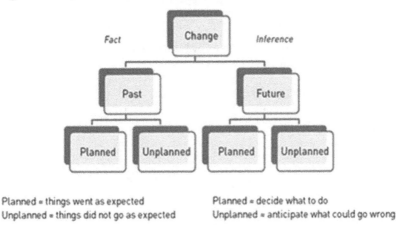

Planned = things went as expected   Planned = decide what to do
Unplanned = things did not go as expected   Unplanned = anticipate what could go wrong

branding when the strategy sets a precedent for how things should be done in the future. An after-action report highlighting areas for improvements and suggestions, if any, helps to guide the strategy making process in the future.

WAYS TO INTRODUCE CHANGE

According to Mintzberg (1987), strategy can be approached as: a plan, a pattern of actions, a position, a perspective, and a ploy. Once the decision makers have decided what needs to be changed, they can introduce the change through:

- *Programs* – steps needed to accomplish a single-use plan (Wheelen & Hunger, 2012). These steps may be structured activities geared toward a specific outcome. For example, an anti-bullying program is a single-use plan of structured activities to address bullying.

- *Initiatives/Campaigns* – single-use plans that may not describe in detail how to achieve outcomes in the implementation phase.

- *Policies* – guiding principles for strategic thinking and decision making that demonstrate intent.

- *Procedures* – sequential steps or techniques that describe in detail how a particular task or job is to be done consistently.

- *Guidelines* – steps that suggest how a particular task or job is to be done but allow contributors to adjust those steps as deemed appropriate without abandoning intent.

- *Recommendations* – suggestions for how a particular task or job should be done.

REACTIONS TO CHANGE

A major barrier to change is how stakeholders react to it. The resistance or unwillingness to change is common. However, a change not wanted by some is often welcomed and desired by others within the same organization. Change starts with the people at the top. Their capacity for accepting and managing change sets the stage for successful organizational change.

Change requires acceptable answers to problems. Draman and Edmondson (2012) pointed out that since the expected set of acceptable answers are framed by the assumptions and beliefs of the questioner, it is easy to see that the parameters for a solution are restricted before the question of *What to Change to?* is asked. If, by some chance, an answer is provided or provided that falls outside the framework of decision makers' and our own mental model (assumptions and beliefs), the answer or the proposed change(s) is often ignored as invalid or too extreme to be applicable. A thinking strategist looks for ways to broaden the mental model of stakeholders through making a strong case for change so that they will change the way they think about the work and will do the work that needs to be done differently. Once the majority of people see the value of the change it can be institutionalized as the way of doing things.

OVERCOMING RESISTANCE TO CHANGE

A thinking strategist is challenged with showing the value of ideas while the stakeholders can only imagine the possibilities. In the planning phase, failure to carefully consider concerns, misconceptions, and points of resistance of stakeholders who have opposing interests may hinder your efforts if one or more of them fails to cooperate or chooses not to go along with (challenge) the plan. Their unwillingness to cooperate or their willingness to challenge your plan raises their stakes. Some might argue that if one individual stakeholder within a group of stakeholders will not cooperate; the firm should just find another one that will. While severing ties seems to be the easy fix to this problem, a thinking strategist ponders the impact of replacement prior to taking this course of action. The only time this is a simple solution is when both parties agree that cooperation is not possible. If it is possible, (the transaction costs are not too high for one or both parties) then both parties should seek to continue the relationship.

Without question, it takes time for parties with opposing interests to become amenable to new ideas. Expect them to be resistant in the beginning. Overcoming resistance requires a demonstration of genuine concern, information that matters to the stakeholder(s), and in most cases, patience, and diligence. As noted by Chesbrough and Teece (1996), cooperation between organizations and others in their industry is necessary for success. Expect cooperation if you can show why actively engaging is in their best interest to do so. Every analysis should consider stakeholder interests. Presentations to the decision makers should reveal how you plan to address stakeholder concerns with three outcomes in mind:

1) gaining their cooperation (play an active role as needed);

2) gaining their agreement to not challenge the plan if they are not a non-factor (their cooperation is not needed or possible); and

3) overcoming challenges to the perceived pitfalls or actions that are deemed to negatively impact stakeholder interest(s).

This process may require negotiations with different stakeholders. Favors may be called in or offered to achieve the desired outcomes. Emotions may run high, but it is your aim to allow those emotions to get people thinking about what could happen if things change or if things stay the same when change is necessary.

For Your Toolbox

Change can be scary. Think of a time when you were initially hesitant to do something different. Did you change your mind? How did you convince yourself that changing the way you think about this issue was in your best interest? How has this thinking helped or hindered you when things mattered to you? How have you evolved over time?

6

CRITERIA FOR CRAFTING
A GOOD STRATEGY

Edmondson and Munchus (2007) point out that strategy is just as much about what organizations decide not to do, as it is what they decide to do. The authors note that at best, decision makers identify all known alternatives, predict accurately all the relevant (short term and long term) consequences, and consistently select the most preferred alternative. Let us explore some of the factors that affect an organization's ability to craft a good strategy.

ACHIEVE GOALS MEET OBJECTIVES

Phase 4, setting financial and strategic objectives drives the strategy managing process. The terms "goal" and "objective" are often used interchangeably in business and may be considered synonymous depending on how those at the table were introduced to these terms. For those who make a distinction between the terms, think of a goal as the purpose for working toward something better. Refer back to the steps of the strategic management process. Coming up with a goal is the focus of Phase 1. Problems represent the need to take action and start work; goals represent the end of work and the need to look for a new problem to solve because the desired state has been reached. There are two kinds of goals:

- An *overarching organizational goal* represents "the ideal" and helps to inform the subsequent stages of the strategy making process. It has no time constraint on when the desired state will happen.

- An *immediate goal* is constrained by a time span put in place by management.

Conversely, think of an objective as something you want to accomplish. Remember, objectives are the focus of Phase 4 of the process. An objective is not conceptually tied to a problem. Objectives are tied to the expectations of results in key areas (sometimes based on past results) and spell out what you want to accomplish by following a process or using a particular strategy. The firm could have met expectations or done well in the last reporting cycle, but it is top management's responsibility to set the expectations for the next reporting cycle.

FINANCIAL AND STRATEGIC PERFORMANCE OBJECTIVES

Performance is the actual result that is accomplished once the strategy has been implemented. If the company meets its objective then performance = objectives. However, performance could be less than the objective or better than the objective. Therefore, there should be agreement regarding the criteria that will be used to determine performance before the strategy is implemented.

Performance objectives are set at each level within an organization. They are based on the structural conditions in which an organization operates, its resources and capabilities (what it can do), and the strategic mindset (willingness to take risks) of the decision makers. Two types of performance objectives are needed:

- *Financial objectives* – target outcomes that relate to improving the company's financial or monetary situation.

- *Strategic objectives* – target outcomes that will result in greater competitiveness and a stronger long-term market position.

Some at the table may judge the objectives as aiming too low or too high. It is essential that the team setting the objectives has been informed by contributors throughout the organization and other stakeholders who are needed to meet the objectives under consideration.

Examples

Financial Objectives (Business/Internally focused):

- Increase earnings growth from 10% to 15% per year.

- Increase ROE (Return on Equity) from 15% to 20%.

- Achieve and maintain an AA bond rating.

Strategic Objectives (Industry/Externally focused):

- Increase market share from 18% to 22%.

- Attain lower costs than rivals.

- Become the industry leader in new product introductions.

Rather than simply proposing objectives to be accomplished, using a SMART approach to setting objectives ensures that everyone knows exactly what the end results should be. SMART is an acronym for:

- Specific – **What?**

- Measurable – **How much?**

- Attainable – **How?**

- Relevant – **Why?**

- Timely – **When?**

Don't get stuck on some of the variations of the acronym S.M.A.R.T. that may surface at the table. For example, you may have already been introduced to the S.M.A.R.T. approach that substituted objectives for goals and used achievable rather than attainable, realistic rather than relevant, tangible rather than timely and may have added an E. for evaluation. Remain flexible so that you can be a contributor in real time. However, always be willing to conduct additional research to learn how these substitutions might play into the strategic management process.

Here's an example using an S.M.A.R.T. Performance Objectives approach for Tori's Southern Kitchen:

The Overarching Organizational Goal – To have the reputation of being the best restaurant throughout the Southeastern part of the United States.

Immediate Goal – Expand into a new market.

Key Result Area – Customer Base.

S.M.A.R.T. Performance Objective:

- Specific – Increase customer base in current markets – **What?**

- Measurable – by 10% (quantify performance) – **How much?**

- Attainable – yes, we have the resources needed or are committed to acquiring them – **How?**

- Relevant – yes, increasing customer base can move us closer to our vision and ultimately to our overarching organizational goal –**Why?**

- Timely – in one year (realistic deadline for achieving results) –**When?**

The objective could be written as *Increase customer base in current markets by 10% in one year* (preference is to show actual date/year). Notice that the statement itself does not reveal whether the objective is attainable or relevant. These two requirements are informed by the environmental analysis from Phase 3 of the strategic management process (see Part II, Chapters 2 and 3) and the mission and vision statement identified in Phase 2, respectively. A narrative would follow that confirms that these two criteria have been considered in the S.M.A.R.T. performance objectives.

RESOURCES AND CONSTRAINTS

As part of an economic system, an organization needs inputs to obtain a desired result (output). For example, people, materials, technology, information, finances are inputs used by businesses. An input can be a resource or a constraint or both. An input is a resource when it increases strategic options and can be used by the firm to compete. An input is a constraint when it does not meet expectations and therefore places limitations on what can be done. More often than not, it cannot be used by the firm to successfully compete. An input can be useful in some situations but not in others.

An honest analysis of inputs is necessary because how an input compares to others in the industry determines whether it is a resource or constraint.

Additionally, an assessment of inputs determines the strategic fit of proposed strategies. Thus, efforts should be made to bring all inputs needed to gain a competitive advantage up to an industry standard or above. The thinking strategist is proficient at finding these inputs, assessing if they can be leveraged or improved, and actually leveraging them when needed, especially when others ignore or simply do not look for ways to use them to gain an advantage. Improving the inputs that create constraints may take time and money, but methodical attention to them may pay off over time. More on overcoming constraints in Part II, Chapter 6.

EVALUATION AND CONTROL

Evaluation of your strategies (consideration of results-performance) takes place internally and externally. Performance can be measured throughout strategy implementation or at the end. If S.M.A.R.T. Performance Objectives are in place, it will be easy to determine whether or not progress is being made toward the objectives when they are met or exceeded. If the objectives were not clearly written, there may be some disagreement about expected outcomes. Thus, it is essential to state how the strategies will be evaluated during the strategy phase when they are crafted.

Your internal stakeholders may have a better idea of how the firm is doing than your external stakeholders. However, until the numbers are reported both base their stance on perceptions, not reality. The strategy could appear to be going well and or the strategy could appear not to be going well but in each case, the numbers may tell a different story. Do not underestimate the value of communicating with key stakeholders throughout the strategy making process. Their valued input serves as an indicator of success.

Regardless of how results are reported, there is some subjectivity in the findings as even computer-generated reports rely on the determinants set by a human to indicate what success looks like. Some people challenge the integrity of using self-reports without corroboration. Observations require signatures from the respondents.

Measuring performance during implementation allows for hands-on control as corrections and corrective actions can be made in real time or before implementation ends. Some decision makers adjust the objectives when it is obvious that failure or not meeting an objective is imminent. It is better not to meet an objective and fully understand why than to take this course of action. As some say, "let it play out" and make only the adjustments to bring about the change you want to see. By letting it play out, the objective may not be met smoothly but the organizational learning that ensues can be beneficial to future decision making sessions and processes. The challenge here is the timing of when to make the adjustments to the strategy so that the objective can be met.

While evaluation can only be done after implementation has begun, control can be considered while the strategy is being crafted. This may be confusing if you learned that decision makers evaluate strategies before they are implemented. The process of considering strategies before they are implemented is analyzing the strategy. An analysis determines value. An evaluation determines success.

For Your Toolbox

Think about other areas that you use strategy. What makes you a strategic thinker in those areas? How were you able to relate some of the content in this chapter with how you currently strategize? What elements can you adapt to become a better strategist using what you already do well?

PART TWO

THE VAULT

SECTION A

TAKING STOCK

Imagine that the tools presented in Part II are secured in a vault that has a combination that is unknown to you. Within this vault are documents and records that contain game-changing practical advice about the best problem-solving practices that can help you advance in your career. You have been given daily access to the contents for the next six months. After that time, you will no longer have access to the vault and thus you will require a solid understanding of each item, its purpose, and when best to use them. Furthermore, you realize that some situations allow you to spend months meticulously using one of the tools and other situations require that you use that tool on-demand "in your head" to respond. Thus, time and effort spent getting comfortable with the processes until they become automatic, intuitive-like, is demanded from you even before the vault is sealed.

1

GATHERING INFORMATION WITH A SHARED GOAL IN MIND

Prior to solving problems, decision makers can make better decisions when they have a complete picture and understanding of the environment in which the organization competes. More than likely, you have met someone who claims that intelligence, intuition, observations, and experience are all you need to make a decision, to solve a problem. Certainly, those four factors add to our ability to make informed decisions. However, good information that goes beyond your own observations is essential to generating ideas about an issue under consideration. Good information considers thoughts about data and experiences outside of our own. How do you get it? By conducting research. Primary research or gathering new information from others who have experience (face-to-face discussions, written surveys, observations, focus groups, etc.) is helpful but can be time-consuming, difficult to administer, and costly. When those dissuading factors and others are of concern, you can seek out secondary research to see what someone else has concluded or deduced about the topic. However, like conducting primary research, there are drawbacks to conducting secondary research. When gathering secondary information, you may find there are thousands of articles and reports written by academics, industry experts and government agencies and only have a short time to read and analyze them. Some documents have industry jargon that you may not understand. Some of them are clearly not written for business practice or to guide the strategy making process. Thus, ensuring that you have a clear picture of relevant factors in the internal and external environment of a firm that most directly frames the window of opportunities and options available is a serious challenge. How do you narrow your search?

How do you get the relevant information you need to be effective? How do you gather the information efficiently? The following points can help you be successful in gathering relevant information irrespective of which approach you use:

SEARCH WITH A SHARED GOAL IN MIND

When searching various information sources for relevant data and information, recognize that others who you rely on for additional insight have a goal in mind when they respond favorably to your request for assistance. Or, they had a goal in mind when they conducted their research. Those goals may or may not be similar to your goal for gathering the information. Understand that each person you talk to, or who responds to a survey, etc., has a goal and each respondent's goals may not mesh well with each other or your reason for conducting the research. A respondent's goal may be simply to "help you succeed," or the company may require mandatory participation, etc. Every document you review has been written with a goal in mind. It may be to convince readers to do something or to highlight problems with a certain innovation. Thus, it is important that you know clearly and define your goal before you begin the research process, that you share your goal with prospective respondents, and gather information with your goal in mind. Most documents or reports will provide an executive summary, abstract, or introduction that explains why the report was written and explains its contribution to knowledge about the topic. This transparency helps to build trust and credibility.

FACT CHECK

You must determine which sources are reliable. While some might argue that consistency is the mark of reliability, information sharing among sources is common. Thus, if a "fact" is reported incorrectly by one source there is a likelihood it will be reported incorrectly in multiple sources unless there is someone questioning the accuracy of the information. Yes, people make mistakes about what is actually happening in a situation, but they also share information that is not absolute. Perhaps not all relevant information was available. Perhaps they intentionally shared inaccurate information. Your role as the thinking strategist is to analyze the information to determine its reliability. Simply put, thinking strategists are "fact checkers" looking for holes in a story that somehow does not add up. Pay close attention to documents and reports shared by firms or research sponsored by a firm. Again, your job is to fact check all documents and reports irrespective of the source. Additionally, a thinking strategist looks for multiple perspectives on the topic.

BENCHMARK BASED UPON STRATEGIC GROUPS

Gathering information about a broad range of competitors can prove to be an exercise in futility. Best practice is to measure a company against its closest rivals: firms that pursue similar strategies with similar resources and objectives. Once you have identified who they are, compare the competitors in the top quartile (choose at least three based on what you want to achieve) to learn more about their strategy and performance over time as conveyed through public information and databases. Also, include a prospector that is not in the top quartile but is gaining momentum and market share. Now, you are better equipped to frame the window of opportunities and options available based on your company's present or proposed strategy and four other competitors.

PAY ATTENTION TO NUMBERS

You might ask why there are many sources of information rooted in finance. Regardless of the spin, the numbers if reported accurately tell the story. They not only explain a company's financial fortitude, but they also can explain how well strategic objectives have been met. Thus, your knowledge of financial statements and skills in analyzing the numbers, and in explaining what the numbers imply to colleagues who may not be as knowledgeable or skilled provide another opportunity for you to contribute to organizational learning, and subsequently firm performance. On the other hand, if you are not strong in this area, take a relevant course. It is well worth the investment for advancing your career.

When analyzing numbers, it is wise to compare numbers among strategic groups. Thompson, Strickland, and Gamble (2008) recommended mapping competitors to reveal which ones are close and which ones are distant. In doing so, companies can learn how well they are doing in comparison to others in the industry. Meeting an objective is bittersweet if you did not do well in comparison to others. Moreover, how well are you doing as a contributor within your company? How well is your unit doing compared to other units at the company? How well are you doing compared to others in your external network who are similarly positioned professionals (same industry, age, background, etc.) and those who are not similarly positioned? Understand that regardless of the publicized picture of an organizational culture that might imply otherwise, internal competition exists. Not only does it exist, but it often motivates people to perform at their best. It may not be necessary to check your outcomes every day or week, but you should check your numbers regularly to determine if adjustments are needed to meet financial and strategic objectives.

Lastly, understand that you can talk to different experts who may give you different interpretations of the numbers and all of them may be right. Thus, you must be very clear about definitions and how you plan to use the information (i.e., to get clarity on firm performance, learn if the firm can exploit industry opportunities, identify any immediate concerns within the firm/industry threats, etc.).

GET READY TO THINK: WHAT YOU THINK REALLY MATTERS

Once you have gathered the relevant information for your decision making process, the need to analyze the information beyond making lists exists. For example, you can brainstorm with your peers to come up with a list of factors that can impact firm performance. However, once the list has been generated, more work is needed. From that point, the team or a responsible member must:

Step 1 is identifying any missing factors that are pertinent to the analysis based on a clearly defined objective.

Step 2 is assessing how each factor impacts firm performance.

Step 3 is determining how each factor interacts with and impacts the other factors.

Step 4 is confronting incongruities and conflict using validating and invalidating data and examples.

Step 5 is assessing the collective strength of the list on firm performance.

Step 6 is examining strategic options based upon the collective strength.

Step 7 is adjusting as needed to gain a competitive advantage.

Failure to move beyond generating lists indicates that the team is not thinking beyond the surface to uncover and understand what is really happening. It is inevitable that statements will be made that are factually inaccurate. It is up to the problem solvers to correct misstatements.

Additionally, do not be afraid to disagree with the group or majority opinion. Engaging in group think or appearing to agree with or going along with the group although you have a dissenting opinion does not ensure that the group is working at optimal capacity. State your concerns so they may be addressed at this point in the process before advancing to another level. There is no guarantee that your opinion will change minds, but depending on your background and thought process, your opinion may increase the diversity of thought/perspectives at the table, raise dissenting opinions, and help to build trust. Thomas and Ely (1996) noted that by challenging basic assumptions (speaking up) about an organization's functions, strategies, operations, practices, and procedures, individuals can help people grow and improve the bottom line. Not speaking up at the table ensures that you have not made an attempt to address the issues that are of concern to you when given a chance to sit at the table. Without considering all sides at the table, the best strategy may be an emergent strategy – one that is unplanned and materializes in the implementation phase. A thinking strategist seeks to ensure that a variety of opinions and insights are considered to identify the best strategy.

Moreover, do not be afraid to disagree with the leader of the group when you have done and can explain the research that supports your stance. Successful leaders should welcome well-supported contributions. However, grandstanding at anyone's expense is never appropriate. If you are concerned that openly voicing a dissenting opinion is not in your best interest, express that you would like to give the topic additional thought. Leaving a meeting with everyone else thinking you are "on board" when you are not can lead to intergroup conflict, inner conflict, and poor strategy execution. However, understand that the time to make decisions (urgency) may not allow for delayed decision making.

Lastly, if you don't have enough facts or have not done the work to offer a well-thought-out contribution to the decision making process (based upon thoughtful analysis of the information prior to the meeting), acknowledge this point and explain how you will contribute to the meeting. "Winging it" is not best practice for a thinking strategist. Here's an opportunity for you to use your critical listening skills to listen closely to every viewpoint, evaluate each perspective carefully, and objectively help those who were prepared make a solid case. Afterward, do the work to be prepared for the next time the topic is addressed.

HANDLING STAKEHOLDER NEED FOR CONFIDENTIALITY

There may be times when you need to gather information that may be controversial or when participating in the information gathering process creates anxiety or tension for prospective respondents. Some people will respond to your request for assistance under expectations of secrecy, primarily confidentiality. They may expect that along with confidentiality comes anonymity. Thus, it is necessary for you to know the difference between confidentiality and anonymity so that you can be transparent in your efforts.

In simple terms, maintaining confidentiality means that only the people conducting the research can with certainty identify the responses of a particular individual. While the researchers may know who participated and how each responded, they should make every effort to prevent anyone not on the team from connecting individuals to their responses. On the other hand, providing anonymity means not even the people conducting the research are able to identify who responded and thus cannot with certainty link individual responses to respondent identities. Therefore, if people agree to a face-to-face meeting with you, then of course you cannot provide anonymity. However, you can and should maintain their confidentiality.

Marking correspondence confidential is not enough to ensure confidentiality. Do not leave confidential information on your desk, on your computer screen, on an unprotected smart device, etc. Do not send an email as

"Confidential" because emails can be forwarded by the sender who may not consider the information confidential.

To protect the identity of people who want to remain anonymous, be willing to use research methods that do not require face-to-face meetings or surveys/questionnaires that do not have identifying information such as:

Name

Addresses

Date (e.g., birthdate, hire date)

Phone/fax numbers

Email addresses

Social security numbers

Employment information

Do not include this information in any notes you take during the session. Likewise, making audio recordings of responses and taking photos of participants violate a person's right to confidentiality/anonymity. Get written permission to do so before using these tactics.

Along these same lines, it is essential that you explain to the respondents how you plan to share your findings with the decision makers. Some respondents may ask to read your report, or at least be provided with the language that you plan to use to tell their story. If requested, you can redact information and comments that can lead to their identity with certainty. Additionally, you can use pseudo names or descriptions as appropriate.

Lastly, there may be a plea for help regarding the stories that are shared based on your perceived insider status. It is important that you demonstrate a concern for their well-being but do not make promises. Your primary method of assisting people will be through the use of the tools presented later in this book.

WILLINGNESS TO ACCEPT FINDINGS

As a thinking strategist, you will need the ability to remain open-minded as you gather information and not fall into what Edward de Bono calls "the intelligence trap": unable to think about new information in an objective way. Without question, if you've developed a system that works for you, the idea that you may have to abandon it for something different, perhaps "unproven," may be daunting and unimaginable. Try not to be trapped by your own intelligence. Don't use it to vigorously defend the status quo or your own preferences.

Objectively consider other points of view and let the evidence lead you to wherever it goes. It may be difficult to do, but don't allow preconceived notions, biases, or assumptions about the topic to hinder your thought process. Report the views of those with whom you disagree and let the decision makers determine which perspective works best given the situation. Remember, you may not have all relevant information about the need for this research, and thus objectively presenting multiple perspectives gives the decision maker more options. Consequently, you are more likely to be considered credible by others who are involved in or are observing the process. Moreover, use your intelligence to craft an organized and clever presentation of the findings likely to win the commitment of the decision makers and those who will be involved in other phases of the process.

For Your Toolbox

What resources are available to you for conducting research? Don't forget about experts you know in the field? If you do not know anyone, create a plan to get to know someone. Identify some magazines and online outlets that provide insights from experts. Be willing to invest in yourself. Pull out those college textbooks. If you did not keep them, reach out to your professors, and ask for the title of the latest edition of the textbook they use.

2

WHAT DOES A COMPANY'S INTERNAL ENVIRONMENT REVEAL ABOUT THE STRATEGY–STRUCTURE RELATIONSHIP?

Karl Ludwig von Bertalanffy's General Systems Theory (1950) notes that all organisms interact with their environments. This biological principle has been adapted to business theories and principles and is a foundational point for environmental analysis used in strategic management, as part of Phase 3. In Chapter 2 of Part I, we briefly discussed how an organizational chart depicts an organizational structure. If you thought an organization chart was only about decision making authority and who reports to whom, think again. Not only does an up-to-date organization chart reveal the structure of an organization, but it also reveals a great deal about its present strategy. If you study the chart, you can tell how many strategic business units the firm has and what products or services it offers. If you don't see more than one unit, then you know it doesn't have a strategy that links all of its units or products and services together. It is not needed. However, if you do see more than one, you might ask why are all of these people and positions needed? How do they get things done? Does it accurately reflect how things "work" inside the industry or business?

The strategy–structure relationship theory set forth by Alfred Chandler in which he argued that structure follows strategy was based on four case studies of industry giants of his time (1962): Du Point, a chemical company, General Motors, an automobile manufacturer, Standard Oil, an energy company, and Sears Roebuck, a retailer. Chandler determined that to give a company the best chance to succeed, an organization's structure should be developed to support strategic approaches. By failing to align structure and strategy, the decision makers put a constraint on firm performance as its structure is not included in its collective strength. It is important to identify the disconnect between strategy and structure in the company's internal environment (Fig. 11).

ORGANIZATIONAL STRUCTURE AND DECISION MAKING

Regardless of whether a company offers one or thousands of products or services, the decision makers (owner(s) or board of directors and top management) set the company's vision, mission, goals, strategic objective, lead the effort to craft and implement supporting strategies, and develop the organizational structure that is deemed to give them the best chances of success. Organizational structure defines how all the parts of an organization work together in the production of products or delivery of services in the industry. The structure is captured in an organization chart which reflects the roles and decision making authority of individuals and the responsibilities of groups or strategic businesses and how they are connected. A strategic

Fig. 11. The Strategy–Structure–Performance Relationship.

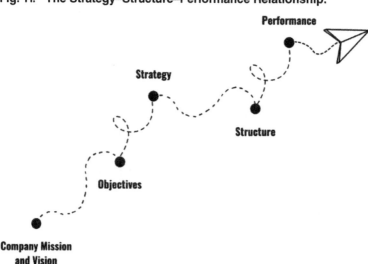

business unit is a fully functional component of a business, having its own functional areas. They can be organized based on geographical area, product lines, or services.

Recall Figs. 1 and 2 that depict two different organization charts. Both charts show the key decision maker(s) at the top and depending on the strategy desired, those roles are followed by either additional layers of managers (reports) or strategic business units. Fig. 1 shows a multiproduct/service structure through the establishments of distinct strategic business units. Fig. 2 shows a single product/service with only one strategic business unit – the entire company is the business unit.

Decision making authority is based on presumptions of where the competency to make decisions lies within the organization. Three kinds of decision making authority exist:

Centralized decision making, expert-based decision making directed by top management or at the executive level.

Decentralized decision making, expert-based decision making directed at the unit or managerial level.

Joint decision making, expert-based decision making is shared by those impacted by the decision.

In a typical structure where multiple strategic business units exist, decisions are decentralized at the product or service level as shown in Fig. 1. A vision statement, mission statements, and performance objectives should be developed for each unit that supports those established by top management. However, within each business unit, the decision making approach may be decentralized or centralized. In a single business structure, as shown in Fig. 2, both centralized and decentralized decision making approaches are common. For sure, the decision on which decision making approach should be not taken lightly as it determines how quickly decisions are made. Moreover, the decision making approach plays a role in the level of commitment of those who are not key decision makers. A top-down approach limits most employee input to the planning phase. A bottom-up approach seeks direct input daily from a broader group of people who have competencies and a presumed need to know how and why decisions are made. Allowing those impacted to give input into the final decision helps to gain commitment and provide a greater sense of individual accountability.

ANALYZING THE INTERNAL SITUATION

We begin by conducting an internal analysis to help determine collective strength, as well as help determine relative strength in the industry as a means of determining what needs to change to gain and subsequently put the firm in a position to leverage a competitive advantage. First, be clear that an internal analysis is not an analysis of a firm's internal stakeholders. Instead, it is an analysis of what is going on inside of the firm and of things that the Board or top management has the authority to control. The aim is to identify resources and competencies that can be acknowledged as strengths and constraints that can be acknowledged as weaknesses. Following are some tools that can help in the process of identifying internal strengths and weaknesses. I recommend completing them in this sequence:

1) A Company Profile

2) Present Strategy Analysis

3) Functional Areas Analysis

4) Competitive Financial Analysis

Once these three analyses have been completed independently, it is then necessary to revisit each to determine how they inform each other and adjust as necessary to identify strengths and constraints.

A COMPANY PROFILE

A company profile is primarily a fact sheet and gives stakeholders a summary of your business. It should include:

Company Name

Headquarter Address

Local Address

Main Phone/Fax Numbers

Company Description

Industry Sic Code(s)

Products and Services

Number of Employees

Number of Locations

Names of Officers, Senior Management

Annual Revenues

Major Competitors

Trends, Developments in Industry

Present Strategy

International Operations

Other Useful Marketing Information (history, awards, social media, etc.)

Website address

PRESENT STRATEGY ANALYSIS

An analysis of a firm's present strategy informs how well the firm is doing at this point in time and helps to determine what needs to change. To start, everyone involved in the strategic management process needs an understanding of three key terms that influence decision making. Paraphrasing theorists de Wit and Meyer (2002):

1. *Strategy content* – describes the change we want to see.

2. *Strategy process* – describes how the change we want to see will be brought about.

3. *Strategy context* – describes the alignment of current conditions with the change we want to see. If the conditions for change are not favorable, the likelihood of failure increases.

Some important questions to consider about the present strategy are:

- What is the present strategy?

- Is it linked to objectives?

- What policies and systems are in place to support the strategy?

- Where is the strategy written down so that problem solvers and contributors can refer to it?

- How is the strategy included in new hire training, development, and HR performance reviews?

- How well is it working to meet the objectives (performance)?

- Has anyone questioned its effectiveness and on what basis?

- What significant changes have occurred or might occur in the future that would influence the company's ability to continue using this strategy?

An undesirable response including "I don't know" to one or more of these questions infers that the structure in place is not inherently tied to strategy. If Chandler is right, then when the strategy changes the structure should change. Moreover, when the strategy is not working, the structure should change. While rising thinking strategists may not have the final say, they can contribute insights into how the structure can be improved.

FUNCTIONAL AREAS OF BUSINESS ANALYSIS

A functional analysis is used to determine how well each function is working to help the firm meet its objectives. A company functions ("works") better when contributors pay attention to details and share how the details matter within an area and to other areas. Business roles are often separated by areas of responsibility referred to as functions such as: accounting, finance, R&D, marketing, human resources, operations/production, and information systems/technology. Each function plays a different but interconnected role in the success of a strategy and a weakness in any one area can harm the collective strength of the company (Fig. 12, Table 2).

Management is not conceptually considered a function of business. Management's role in strategy is to make judgments and decisions about what is best practice or what can and will be done in the functional areas and evaluate success and reward those who meet or exceed expectations.

When examining how well each function is working to help the firm meet its objectives, management decides how functions should be completed

Fig. 12. Functional Areas of Business Along Management Activities.

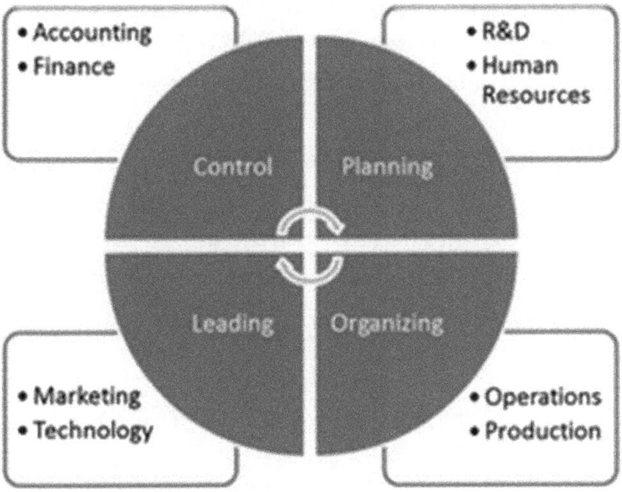

Table 2. Role Business Functions in Crafting and Implementing Strategy.

Business Function	Role in Crafting and Implementing Strategy
Accounting	Depicts quantitatively and provides narrative of how money was spent and provide key financial ratios which determine success
Finance	Ensures the business has enough money for successful strategy implementation
R&D	Creates and tests new products and services
Production	Makes products and services come to reality and meet a standard set by the industry or firm
Information systems	Captures results that can be used to set strategy and monitors results
Operations	Ensures that products and services are delivered efficiently
Human resources	Hires, trains, develops, motivates, evaluates, and terminate people
Marketing	Provides rationale and narrative of how to draw stakeholders to the company and its products and services
Technology	Makes processes work more effectively and efficiently and track progress through automation

(whether through departments or by the same person(s)et.). They may determine that some functions should be outsourced to other firms due to lack of capacity or time constraints; however, this tactic does not alleviate management of its duty to pay attention to the function. Management must effectively determine and communicate the organization's needs, select a results-oriented vendor, manage the relationship, and track results. Some common functions that are outsourced are human resource management, information systems management, and finance/accounting. Although functions that are outsourced cannot be included as a source of the company's collective strength, their decision to use outsourcing can be included.

COMPETITIVE FINANCIAL ANALYSIS

It is pertinent that a financial analysis is conducted prior to assessing company strengths and weaknesses. First, conduct an analysis to determine how well the company is meeting its financial objectives and look for opportunities to improve the numbers. Additionally, try to get financials on other firms available through 10ks, annual reports, and data companies such as Bloomberg and Thomson Reuters. The conclusions drawn from a competitive financial analysis can be included as either a strength or weakness based on industry rank, annual sales or revenues and ratios of select companies within their strategic group. Again, it is essential that companies carefully consider the numbers and not depend on analyses and interpretations offered. See Part II, Chapter 10 for key financial ratios and what they reveal about a firm's strengths and weaknesses.

Pay attention to what is happening in management and in each functional area to identify strengths and weaknesses. Included in this analysis are inputs and outputs, ways of doing things (policies, practices, and processes) and support systems that are purposed to ensure that things get done effectively and efficiently. Strengths are factors about the firm that can be exploited or leveraged to gain a competitive advantage. On the other hand, weaknesses are factors that cannot. Don't err in labeling a factor as a strength or a weakness based on its perception as a resource or a constraint. A resource only becomes a strength when it is compared to similar resources of competitors within a strategic group. Note, however, that a constraint is only a weakness when it is compared to the competitors' resources. If all firms in the analysis

Table 3. Comparison of Firm Relative Strength.

	Firm X (Your Firm Here)	Firm A	Firm B	Firm C	Relative Strength
Resource 1					
Resource 2					
Resource 3					
Constraint 1					
Constraint 2					
Constraint 3					

have the same or similar resources or constraints, those factors are not considered strengths or weaknesses. Those should be considered competitive factors for this strategic group (Table 3).

Nicky Garcea, Stephen Isherwood, and Alex Linley (2011) pointed out that there may be surprises in this analysis, in that through this process, a problem solver may discover strengths that it did not know to exist. Some unrealized strengths emerge in strategy implementation and significantly impact how the remainder of the activities is put into action. Additionally, some weaknesses may be discovered which show that resources and competencies thought to be difference makers are not. Although many experts assert that centering strategy on weaknesses should be abandoned, attention to weaknesses in the appropriate functional areas can lead to improvements in collective strength. For example, if human capital needs development, then an analysis on human resources should provide clarity on the issue and include recommendations on how to address this need.

For Your Toolbox

For the remainder of this textbook, consider how the content applies to your ability to be a trusted, intuitive, and competent team player (i.e., a thinking strategist). At the end of this and each subsequent chapter, connect the advice provided to your current role, while understanding that your aim is to next level. Consider how you are required to collaborate effectively with others to be successful.

3

EVALUATING A COMPANY'S EXTERNAL ENVIRONMENT, THE FIRM–INDUSTRY–SOCIETY RELATIONSHIP

The firm-industry-society-relationship is the core of an unwritten social contract that demands that organizational leaders undertake their economic responsibilities to make a profit while not overlooking their ethical responsibilities to be demonstrate a duty of care and be good corporate citizens. Choosing the right balance means acknowledging the external conditions in which the firm competes.

ANALYZING THE EXTERNAL ENVIRONMENT

In addition to analyzing the internal environment in which the company has control, as part of Phase 3, problem solvers and contributors also identify the possible opportunities and threats over which the company has little control to complete the environmental analysis. Identifying industry opportunities and threats can be challenging for one reason: the experts cannot agree on the definition of industry opportunities or threats. Some capture industry opportunities as potential strategies that a company can use to compete. Others view opportunities as the positive conditions in demographic, sociocultural, political/legal, technological, economic, and global factors in an industry that could lead to changes in strategy.

I agree with the latter view that stipulates that opportunities and threats are not specific to a firm in an industry. A good caveat is if a named firm can be inserted into the statement it is unlikely to be an opportunity and more likely to be a strategy. For example, entering new markets, developing new products, creation of a distribution network are examples of strategies that one or more firms can use to compete. Therefore, you could easily insert the name of a company when listing these factors: XYZ can enter into new markets, develop new products, create a distribution network, etc.

However, opportunities and threats for an industry are not tied to a particular firm, they are industrywide. For example, a problem unresolved (unfulfilled customer need), changes in consumer preferences, more people getting college degrees, growing population in urban areas, increase in strategic partnerships, a market vacated by an ineffective competitor, fewer government regulations, and global economic activity.

Likewise, threats are negative conditions in demographic, sociocultural, political/legal, technological, economic, and global factors in an industry. Examples are changes in consumer preferences (can be both an opportunity and a threat), industry slowdown caused by difficult economic times, increase in energy costs, fewer natural resources in a region, technologies that require substantial investment, adverse government policies, and variances in international judicial systems.

Given the variance in business capability, a company will perceive the pressures of these conditions differently. Each should weigh its own resources and constraints in light of opportunities and threats to determine to what degree an opportunity or threat impacts its success.

Again, given the enormity of this task, narrowing the analysis to strategic groups can make it less daunting. Following are some analytical tools that can also help. I recommend you complete them in this sequence:

1. Six Segment General Environment Analysis

2. External Driving Forces Analysis

3. Stakeholder Power Analysis (More thorough analysis of each stakeholder)

4. Comprehensive SWOT Analysis (Revisit all analyses internal and external analyses and adjust as necessary)

5. SWOT Analysis

SIX SEGMENT GENERAL ENVIRONMENT ANALYSIS

Business cannot ignore what is happening in the broader society or its general environment. To be successful, problem solvers must consider what is happening now and what could change. As conveyed in Table 4, within the general environment are six segments: demographic, sociocultural, political/legal, technological, economic, and global. This analysis is also referred to as a STEEP or PESTEL analysis.

Just like the functional areas of business, each segment should be analyzed to determine what is going on and how it has the potential to impact strategy. It is highly unlikely that a segment would have no impact on a strategy. Additionally, as noted by Dess, Lumpkin, and Taylor (2005), a given trend or event may have a positive impact on some industries and a negative or neutral impact or none at all on others.

Thus, a strategy-based Six Segment Analysis of the General Environment can help determine and improve the chances of success. Look for the following:

- Trends in each segment that have positive and negative implications for the industry and your company. Consider how and why each trend will impact society, your industry, your company, defender strategy types, and your closest rivals.

- Contradictions between the trends. Consider those contradictions within the context of your competitive environment.

- Advantages that can be exploited in future strategies. Consider your resources (talent, time, and money).

Table 4. The General Environment.

Demographic	Factors that identify and distinguish a target population or market (age, race, gender, income, etc.)
Sociocultural	Factors relating to society's attitudes and cultural values
Political/Legal	Government policies, laws, and regulations that impact a particular industry
Technological	Technology available or needed for business operations
Economic	The role the economy plays in business decisions (wages, interest rates, etc.)
Global	Existing global markets and the opportunity for the development of new markets

- Conflicts or dilemmas caused by your constraints. Consider how they will affect planned future strategies.

This analysis can also show how each of the segments impact the firm and will inform the SWOT Analysis. Those that have positive implications are shown as opportunities and those that have negative implications are identified as threats.

EXTERNAL DRIVING FORCES ANALYSIS

For years, Michael Porter's (1979) Five Forces Model has been used as a strategic tool to help analyze the competitiveness and attractiveness of a market:

(1) the intensity of rivalry among competitors;

(2) threat of new entrants;

(3) bargaining power of suppliers;

(4) bargaining power of the buyers; and

(5) the threat of substitute products and services.

Two additional forces have been added: complementors and the other stakeholders. Complementors were added to the model by businessman Andy Grove (1996) who defined them as other businesses from whom customers buy complementary products. He noted that each company's products work better or sometimes only works with the other company's product (p. 29). Additionally, Thomas Wheelen and David Hunger (2012) acknowledge the role that other stakeholders play in driving competition and profits in an industry. They identified the first seven stakeholders below and I added the eighth for clarity:

(1) governments (it is imperative that contributors in the firm know which agency has oversight over their industry and the rules pertaining to the business function(s) they perform for the firm);

(2) local communities;

(3) creditors (if not included with suppliers);

(4) trade associations;

(5) special interest groups;

(6) unions (if not included with suppliers);

(7) shareholders (or owners); and

(8) end users (if not same as buyers).

The analysis of the firm's relationship with these 14 and other stakeholders is based on the comparison with the other firms in the same industry. As a result of this analysis, not only can decision makers determine industry attractiveness, but they can use the knowledge gained in the analysis to assess several and identify the optimal strategic option.

FORCES DRIVING INDUSTRY COMPETITION AND ATTRACTIVENESS

Most theorists do not place a weight on which of the factors have more relevance in the analysis (Fig. 13, Table 5). However, Coulter (2013) notes that given the time it takes to do an analysis, paying more attention to critical sectors (key result areas) and less attention to other sectors is the key to making the process as efficient and effective as possible.

Fig. 13. Driver of Industry Profits 1.

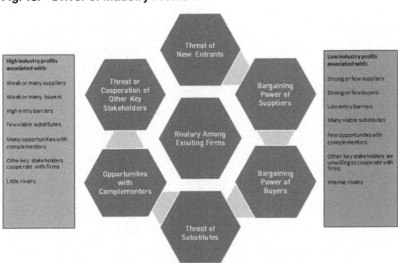

Table 5.   The Driving Forces of Industry Competition.

Rivalry among existing firms	How many competitors and how intense is the competition between companies that offer the same or similar products and services (strategic group)?
Threat of new entrants	What is the likelihood that a new competitor can thrive in this industry?
Bargaining power of suppliers	What leverage do companies that supply materials or resource inputs to the industry – may not be the end user – have in economic transactions? Be specific, name suppliers?
Bargaining power of buyers	What leverage do companies that purchase or use outputs (products or services) have in economic transactions? Be specific, name buyers?
Threat of substitutes	What other ways can a customer solve the problem other than using the companies that compete within this industry?
Opportunities with complementors	What partnerships can be forged between companies that have products, services that buyers often, or could conceptually tie together (peanut butter and jelly)?
Threat or cooperation with other key stakeholders	What role do other key stakeholders not explicitly covered already in the analysis play in the success or failure of this industry?

STAKEHOLDER POWER ANALYSIS

Within each function within an organization are problem solvers and contributors working together to meet the needs of, and therefore attract internal stakeholders, as well as to exercise some level of control in how external stakeholders respond to strategy. Thus, a strategy-based stakeholder power analysis helps to determine and improve the stakeholder relationships identified in the External Driving Forces Analysis.

Such analysis can be completed through a seven-step process:

Step 1 is making a list of relevant stakeholder types (include both internal and external).

Step 2 is explaining the role that each type plays in a typical economic transaction.

Step 3 is explaining the realistic expectations of each type in everyday decision making.

Step 4 is identifying the *actual stakeholders* within each category type.

Step 5 is using the following legend to describe each stakeholder's power balance in an industry.

 a. P = powerful (has power and is likely to use it)

 b. A = average (may have power but not a threat in the industry))

 c. L = less powerful (may be vulnerable)

Step 6 is using the following legend to describe the business relationship with each stakeholder

 d. C = cooperates as needed

 e. O = opposes plans

 f. X = unpredictable (may be persuaded to act in a given situation)

Step 7 is determining where opportunities for cooperation exist in this current business endeavor.

As a result of this analysis, problem solvers can write out scenarios of how the company and the stakeholder might interact when a proposed change is under consideration. As shown in Fig. 14, the problem solver should revisit all previous internal and external analyses and make adjustments as necessary to capture a complete picture of the situation. This comprehensive analysis will inform the SWOT Analysis

SWOT ANALYSIS

The information analyzed in the previous analyses informs the SWOT Analysis – a comprehensive analysis that examines the strengths and weaknesses of the company and the opportunities and threats of the industry to provide a systems view of what is happening in today's reality. The SWOT analysis is presented in four quadrants and shows a list of factors that are considered strengths, weaknesses, opportunities, and threats (Fig. 15). While a company's strengths lead to competitive advantages, its weaknesses lead to competitive disadvantages.

Fig. 14.   Driver of Industry Profits 2.

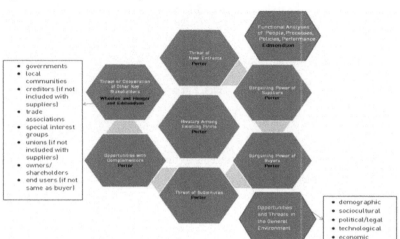

Fig. 15.   SWOT Analysis.

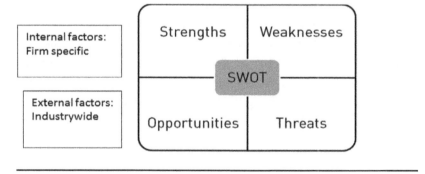

There are four steps to creating a SWOT Analysis:

Step 1 is considering the information gathered from previous analyses.

Step 2 is placing the factors into the correct SWOT quadrant. When a factor is both a strength and a weakness or both an opportunity and a threat; it should be listed as both. Thus, each factor should be written as a complete statement (Fig. 16).

Fig. 16.   Example of Step 1 in a SWOT Analysis.

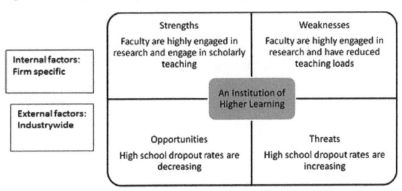

Step 3 is identifying the strategies that can be used to gain a competitive advantage through matching in a TOWS matrix.

Step 4 is clearly stating the competitive advantages and disadvantages of using each strategy:

To look for competitive advantages (Table 6):

> *Match Strengths and Opportunities*
>
> *Match Strengths and Threats*

To look for competitive disadvantages (Table 6):

> *Match Weaknesses and Opportunities*
>
> *Match Weaknesses and Threats*

As shown in Table 7, it is not uncommon to see a SWOT Analysis where ONLY steps 1 and 2 are shown. These analyses offer *strategic options* that a particular firm can pursue rather than external opportunities found in the general environment.

In these cases, some people around the table may be able to isolate the steps while others cannot. Thus, a thinking strategist must be able to look at the results of an analytical tool and think of steps that may have not been

Table 6.   Example of Step 2 – The SWOT Strategies Matrix.

SWOT Strategies Matrix		
	Strengths	Weaknesses
Opportunities	S/O strategies	W/O strategies
Threats	S/T strategies	W/T strategies

Table 7.   Common Mistakes in a SWOT Analysis.

S/O *strategies* presented as Opportunities	W/O or W/T *strategies* presented as Threats
Open 3 new international offices	Patent our inventions

included or discussed to ensure that those steps are not ignored in a process. Moreover, based on what is revealed in the analysis, the thinking strategist can begin to determine what needs to be changed to better reflect the situation and explain why the change is needed to the other stakeholders at the table.

Next, consider the situational background for an example that will be used for the remainder of this book to help demonstrate how to use the problem-solving tools in the strategic management process.

AN OVERVIEW OF SKYE CONSTRUCTION

Skye Construction, a privately held firm, operates in three states in the Southeastern part of the United States (Georgia, South Carolina, and North Carolina). The company serves primarily as a subcontractor for larger construction companies including developers that build luxury high rises in communities that include entertainment, shopping, and dining. Top management is concerned that they have experienced a loss in contracts and productivity that eventually led to a loss in revenue. Committed to turning this situation around, they created an internal task force charged with identifying growth opportunities.

An attempt was made to ensure that the task force was composed of a diverse team of problem solvers and contributors from different backgrounds and at various levels in seven departments: Accounting, Sales, Marketing, Operations, IT, Human Resources, and Finance. In their first meeting, under fire from the board, the CEO informed them that he would like to see the company expand into at least two more states within two years. First, he wants to understand what is going on now so that the issues can be addressed before recommending expansion. He emphasized that resources would be allocated to support their planning efforts.

Having seen the financial numbers; the task force left the meeting a little cautious but ready to work. They began with what they knew best: a look into what was happening inside the company.

ENVIRONMENTAL FACTORS

This business enjoys several strengths that collectively could lead to a competitive advantage. Skye Construction has been around for more than 35 years and unlike its competitors, has simple mission and vision statements, along with a catchy slogan that informs stakeholders:

Mission statement: Skye Construction is a commercial builder of LEED-designed structures.

Vision Statement: Skye Construction will be the most sought-after construction-services provider in the Southern part of the United States.

Slogan: Skye Is The Limit!

The construction industry is project based. Their knowledge in building LEED (Leading in Energy and Environmental Design) projects is unsurpassed in the region. Their brand is strong, and they work closely with their partners to meet delivery schedules, do quality work, and fulfill other terms of their contracts. Thus, they depend on repeat business and maintenance contracts. Fifteen years ago, they purchased a small company that provided some of the raw materials needed for their construction jobs and that acquisition has paid off. Five years later, they expanded their work to include masonry. Other firms in their strategic group are resource dependent on suppliers. Skye Construction has been recognized for its diversity and inclusion efforts and has a philanthropic foundation that is well known in the Charlotte area.

The CEO is a former VP of a construction unit for a huge service provider in Cleveland, Ohio and was responsible for bringing in a $7billion contract to build two operations centers that would serve over 11,000 restaurants prior to leaving. With an MBA from UNC-Chapel Hill, he has been able to transfer that knowledge and experience to Skye Construction. Since moving to Charlotte, North Carolina, to take the helm as the CEO about six months ago, he has made some key hires in the C-Suite. He holds weekly conference calls with the VPs and holds onsite quarterly meetings on a rotating basis. Moreover, he is regularly recruited by firms as a turnaround strategist.

Although the company has been around for over 35 years, Skye Construction is considered relatively young in the industry. Their strategic partners are mainly in Charlotte where Skye Construction headquarters is located. The company also has offices in Atlanta, Georgia, and Greenville, South Carolina, and a total of 103 employees. Top management has not reached out or made concerted efforts to respond to partners in rural areas or other states. Nor has it expanded the reach of its foundation beyond the Charlotte area. The website has information from three years ago listed as current news and they have no social media presence. Thus, the company has not positioned itself to increase the number of strategic partnerships needed to gain economies of scale that would allow it to expand into two other states (Fig. 17).

Moreover, a financial analysis showed only two straight years of positive earnings in the last five years. While its asset base is growing, revenues are declining (down $30mil from previous year). Additionally, Skye Construction's cost structure is higher than its rivals are, and the CEO has pledged to find ways to bring it in line with the industry average to get more developers to go green.

Some competitors exited the industry during an economic downturn and a slowdown in the housing market. The construction companies that survived found themselves in a highly competitive construction business environment. However, the construction industry is rebounding given both federal and state spending to improve infrastructure as a way to inject money

Fig. 17. Financial Analysis of Skye Construction.

Financial Analysis

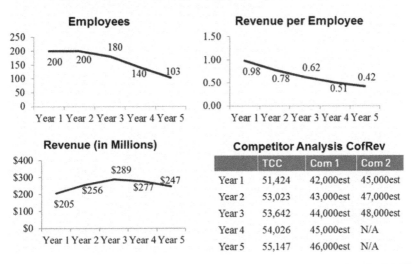

	TCC	Com 1	Com 2
Year 1	51,424	42,000est	45,000est
Year 2	53,023	43,000est	47,000est
Year 3	53,642	44,000est	48,000est
Year 4	54,026	45,000est	N/A
Year 5	55,147	46,000est	N/A

into the economy. Firms in the geographical areas that Skye Construction competes in are taking advantage of the increased level of economic activity. The weather has been favorable, and LEED is becoming the industry standard. Raw materials are cheaper and drive down costs.

4

GAINING ALIGNMENT ON WHAT IS HAPPENING AND WHY

The tools problem solvers use to analyze the current situation point out some of the things that management is doing well. They also point out some of the undesirable outcomes of their decision making. When things are not as desired, managers often disagree on where the problem lies or what is causing it, and therefore need a method to understand how particular business practices and industry phenomena are leading to undesirable outcomes.

In this chapter, a modified version of the use of a Current Reality Tree (CRT), a tool from the Theory of Constraints (TOC), will be used to paint a clear picture of what is actually happening and what should be happening in a situation. The TOC is a systems thinking approach to solving problems. As indicated in the previous chapter, TOC emphasizes that to effectively analyze a problem, the problem solvers should consider the entire system in which a company operates. Although CRTs are one of five logic diagrams in TOC, it can be used as a standalone process to help answer the question *What to change?* about an existing situation.

CURRENT REALITY TREES

Constructing a CRT to depict what is going on in a company requires input from stakeholders throughout the system. If people do X, then Y will happen. However, in decisions that involve systems with many intermingling parts, causal links are frequently unclear. Thus, meetings with various stakeholders are held to brainstorm about what is happening –what is not working as planned, in particular – in their eyes. These meetings are not held to resolve the problem but to ensure that when the meetings are concluded, the problem (what needs to be *and* can be improved with better decision making) has been thoroughly discussed across stakeholder groups.

During these meetings, often referred to as brainstorming sessions, the pertinent points the participants will make frequently do not describe outcomes that are desired by a company; instead, these observations are considered undesirable effects (UDEs). UDEs are visible results that are not in line with what ought to be happening throughout the system if the system was working ideally or even adequately. Thus, it is important that the note-taker records each participant's input accurately and that the facilitator asks probing questions to ensure that the message has been communicated effectively and encourages participants to provide clarification as needed after the meeting.

Not only should the participants inform the facilitator of what is happening, but also based on their specialized expertise, a presumed cause of why it is happening. These statements become part of the cause-and-effect logic used to link the UDEs later.

Tracey Burton-Houle (2000) noted that a well-written UDE: (1) is a complete statement; (2) identifies an effect that can be changed (without the presumed cause); (3) precisely identifies a condition that exists in today's reality; (4) is something negative or undesirable in its own right; (5) does not include a presumed solution; and (6) describes a single effect that needs no clarification by such words as "and," "because," "due to," or "as a result."

In addition to correctly noting UDEs, a problem solver has to spell out the presumed causes that may have led to them. By using the presumed causes that were mentioned in the brainstorming session(s), as well as any presumed causes that may have surfaced in the analysis, the problem solvers should be able to determine if the UDE is presumed to be caused by a business practice or it if is presumed to be caused by an industry factor that management cannot solve on its own. If it is presumed to be caused by a business practice, then the problem solver should attempt to identify within what functional area the problem first surfaces. If it is presumed to be caused by an industry factor, then the problem solvers should have an idea where within the system (in the internal or external environment) the problem becomes an issue for another stakeholder as well. When a factor impacts a few and not most firms within the industry, it cannot strongly be considered an industry factor, and internal analysis should be considered (Table 8).

Table 8. Five Requirements for Analyzing UDEs.

What Should Be Happening	Undesirable Effects	Where Is the UDE Visible to Stakeholder(s)?	Stakeholder Type	Where Is the Presumed Solution (s)?
Desired outcome	UDE 1	Stakeholder	I or E	Functional area
Desired outcome	UDE 2	Stakeholder	I or E	Functional area
Desired outcome	UDE 3	Stakeholder	I or E	Functional area
Desired outcome	UDE 4	Stakeholder	I or E	Functional area

To tie the UDEs together and to determine whether a presumed cause is an actual cause, a sufficiency or necessity logic statement is carefully crafted. Sufficiency and necessity logic show implicational relationships between two or more statements or conditions (UDEs; Fig. 18):

Like connecting speakers to audio equipment with a single-wire electrical connector called a banana, conditions within a necessity clause are connected with a circle called a "banana."

If there is a gap in logic or understanding between the UDEs and the causes, then the problem solvers will need to fill in the gaps by adding additional points to turn what appeared to be a sufficiency clause into a necessity clause or adding another UDE and associated sufficiency and necessity

Fig. 18. Sufficiency and Necessity Clauses.

Sufficiency Clause	
If one statement can cause another statement to be true, then it is a sufficiency clause. If A then B is a sufficiency clause = if then	Then If
Necessity Clause	
If two or more statements are needed to cause another statement to be true, then it is a necessity clause. If A and B then C is an necessity clause = if and then	Then If And
Note: A banana is a connector used for joining wires to equipment. This term is used to represent the oval (shown above) that connects entities in a necessity clause.	

clauses. As noted by Cox, Blackstone, and Schleier (2003), not all of the possible causes of an effect have to be identified – enough causes that can account for 80% or more is sufficient. When you are done, you should be able to tell a convincing story about each UDE and how it impacts the larger story about what is happening in the company.

Next, let us explore how a CRT can be used to gain stakeholder alignment on the problem to be solved in Skye Construction.

FINDINGS FROM SKYE CONSTRUCTION

Again, the task force went to work immediately after meeting with the CEO. They held brainstorming sessions with both internal and external stakeholders to understand the decisions that led to the current reality that needs to be addressed.

IDENTIFYING UDEs

The information in the text blocks in Fig. 19 represents some of the issues described by the contributors. The contributor assigned to develop the CRT first removed the points that were not germane to the issue and later isolated content so that each note represented a single thought or UDE. Only those statements that were relevant would be captured in the CRT.

DEVELOPING A CRT

Two kinds of CRTs are used in organizations: internal facing CRTs and external facing CRTs. Fig. 20 is an example of an internal facing CRT. It would not be presented in a meeting with those who were not present in the brainstorming session. Fig. 21 is an example of an external facing CRT, which would be presented in a meeting with those who were not present in the brainstorming session.

The numbers on Figs. 19 and 20 represent the order that the statements were made in the brainstorming session(s). While these numbers are useful

Fig. 19. List of UDEs.

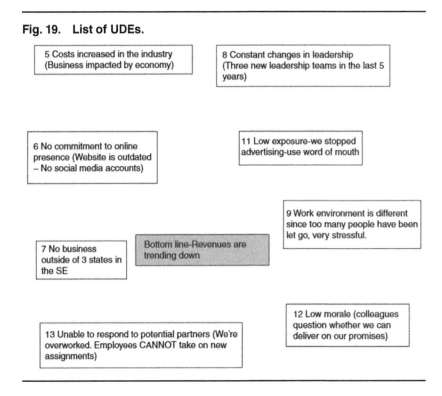

in reading CRTs in preparation for presenting your external facing CRT, it is highly improbable that a decision maker is interested in trivialities and thus, those numbers are not shown in an external facing CRT (Fig. 21).

Someone covering an internal CRT could start with 6 and 7 or with 4 then 5.

Someone covering an external CRT would simply tell a story based on what is in the text boxes the given numbers have been deleted.

THE FOLLOW-UP MEETING

The internal task force met with the CEO and other members of top management to discuss their findings that outline where problems lie with Skye Construction's present strategy. As recommended by the VP of Operations during one of the team's meetings with key stakeholders, the team presented the findings in an external facing CRT.

Fig. 20.   Internal Facing CRT.

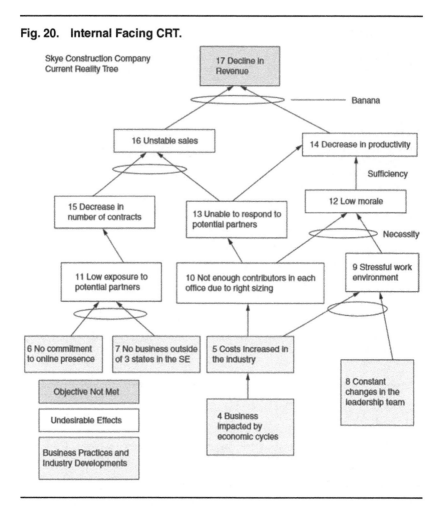

SEVEN KEY POINTS

1. As a thinking strategist, listen to understand during the brainstorming sessions. Observing the situation in real time allows for better understanding and reassures the participants that you want to fully understand their concerns prior to resolving the issue. Include other problem solvers in critical business functions in these observations for better results.

Fig. 21.   Components of an External Facing CRT.

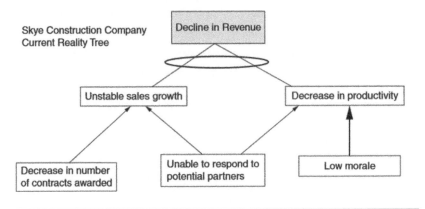

An acceptable order to start reading with 6 and 7:	An acceptable order to start reading with 4 then 5:
If 6 and 7 then 11	If 4 then 5
If 11 then 15	If 5 and 8 then 9
If 4 then 5	If 5 then 10
If 5 and 8 then 9	If 10 and 9 then 12
If 5 then 10	If 12 then 14
If 10 and 9 then 12	If 10 then 13
If 12 then 14	If 13 then 14
If 10 then 13	If 6 and 7 then 11
If 13 then 14	If 11 then 15
If 13 and 15 then 16	If 13 and 15 then 16
If 16 and 14 then 17	If 16 and 14 then 17

2. The UDE at the top of the CRT is the most important UDE; it represents the end result of all UDEs (objective not met). When reporting, the main objective that is not met should be communicated as a complete problem statement and the strategic intent moving forward. For example, the CRT revealed that Skye Construction is experiencing a decline in revenue as evidenced by a decrease in productivity and unstable sales growth. The next step is to determine how best to resolve one or both of those constraints to reverse the decline in revenue.

3. Rather than "tree," always refer to a CRT by its complete name or as a CRT given in the Theory of Constraints five of the six logic diagrams are "trees": CRT, Future Reality Tree, Prerequisite Tree, Strategy & Tactics Tree, and Transition Tree. The remaining logic diagram is the Conflict Cloud.

4. It may be necessary for the contributor who develops the CRT to add an entity that was not discussed by the participants in the brainstorming session to connect them in meaningful ways. Relevant observations from external and internal analyses should also be included in the CRT.

5. When telling the story – the story should be told from the bottom to the top of the CRT. Moreover, "If-then" and "If and then" statements are only used when building or reading the contents of the CRT and therefore should be eliminated when telling the story. Even when covering an internal CRT, the numbers are not mentioned, only the content.

6. The story should flow like any other story you would tell. If you jump from one side of the CRT to the other, your story will not flow well. Complete your thought by going as far up the CRT as possible on one side before going to the other side.

7. An effective way to tell the story is with a visual that depicts the worst-case scenario. This approach will help to capture the attention of your audience and evoke emotions that can overcome resistance to change.

SECTION B

CRAFTING STRATEGY FOR COMPETITIVE ADVANTAGE

The aim of the strategy making process is not to come up with *the* strategy but to continuously strategize or craft strategies to improve performance and avo6id potential problems. Over time, a company's approach to crafting strategy and the resulting strategy becomes its identity within the industry and affects its future opportunities. Again, not everyone is "cut out" to work in an industry or at a particular company within the industry. Finding a company that uses a strategic approach that you can contribute to with confidence based on your working style and level of creativity is essential to your long-term success.

5

THEORY LINKING STRATEGY TO PERFORMANCE OBJECTIVES

Just as structure follows strategy, strategy follows objective. The strategic management process centers on crafting and implementing strategies to achieve objectives and outperform the competition. Prior to crafting the strategy, management (with board approval) develops the company's vision and mission for the company. They also set the long-term and short-term strategic objectives that must be met. Once the objective has been shared, a strategy with that objective as its epicenter becomes the focus of all activities in each strategic business unit and functional area. There is no general inherent advantage in implementing one strategy over another. The strategy chosen should be based on the objectives that an organization wants to achieve and the resources available to achieve them (e.g., structure, talent, material goods). What works for one firm may not work for another and shown in Fig. 22, the process is dynamic rather than linear.

COMPETITION AND SUSTAINABILITY

There really is no difference in how competition is viewed in business than it is in other situations. As in any competition, there is an activity that is undertaken by two or more participants that are considered rivals. The rivals are battling for a prize (usually identified and agreed upon before the competition begins) and the one who does the best in the activity wins

Fig. 22. The Dynamic Strategy–Structure–Performance Relationship.

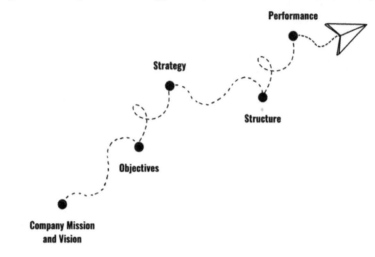

the prize. A participant can be disqualified based on behavior or can quit the competition, but even so, there is usually a winner. In some cases, the competition may end in a tie, which means the prize or winnings are shared. In some cases, there is no clear winner; maybe there is even disagreement about who won.

Sustainability implies that competition is not a one-time occurrence. Nonetheless, there is a participant that is so much better than its competition that this participant wins time and time again. Moreover, winning a few games is not the goal; the goal is to win the championship and back-to-back titles. While there is a likelihood that the participant will lose at least one or two games in a series, their collective strength is unmatched. Again, competitive strength is the interdependencies of factors, both positive and negative, that determine competitive positioning. As a result of interdependencies, there is a perception of the relative strength a firm has compared to its competitors within an industry. If it helps, remember that sports is an industry. The teams represent the firms. The players are problem solvers and contributors, the coaches are top management, the owners are the board, the fans are the buyers, etc. Due to the unmatched collective strength of their leadership, their workout facility, their practice patterns, even though they may have lost a game during the regular season, etc., they are a team to beat and have a competitive advantage. Teams that made it to the finals or have multiple championship rings within a three- to four-year period have a sustainable competitive advantage.

LEVERAGING COMPETITIVE ADVANTAGE FOR AN EDGE

Competitive positioning may include: competitive parity, which indicates that the firm's resources are valuable but not rare for the industry; distinctive competence, which indicates that the firm has resources that lead to its ability to deliver a product better/faster than rivals; competitive advantage, which indicates that the firm's strengths put it in a favorable or superior business position to leverage industry opportunities; and competitive disadvantage, which indicates that the firm's weaknesses put it in an unequal and unfavorable business position to face industry threats. A firm is said to have a competitive advantage when its collective strength cannot be matched by other firms in the industry. However, only if leveraged well will unmatched collective strength give a firm an edge and put the other firms at a disadvantage. Likewise, a firm is said to be at a competitive disadvantage when it lacks something essential for success or its collective strength cannot match the collective strength of other firms in the industry. The firm that has the better collective strength must be able to identify its competitive advantage and use it to its advantage when crafting and implementing strategies. For example: a firm that holds a competitive advantage based on the collective strength in its cost structure due to efficient production techniques or economies of scale has more options in setting its selling price. It can set its desired selling price lower, the same, or higher than others for higher margins (difference in cost and desired selling price). Alternatively, a firm can hold a competitive advantage based on quality, perception, or branding, etc., which means it can charge more for its products. If they don't leverage their competitive advantage, firms that cannot match it are not at a competitive disadvantage. Depending on the competition, a firm may have a competitive advantage with one set of competitors and be at a competitive disadvantage with another set of competitors.

The idea of leveraging collective strength can be traced back to Peter Drucker (1967) who pointed out that the unique purpose of an organization is to make strength productive. The value of having a competitive advantage resides in the fact that it signals to others that a firm is powerful and, hence a good partner to do business with or it signals that a firm should not be ignored. Competitive advantage is valuable when it is visible and acknowledged by key stakeholders and should be leveraged for all it is worth.

After a huge upset in sports, pundits spend days disclosing the flaws in decision making of the team that was expected to win but blew it, and teams agonize over losing a game when they should be celebrating. While the "underdog" may have been underestimated, they realize that with talent and good decision making they could win. Never hold a competitor in awe to the degree that you are afraid to compete. Moreover, don't hold one person in awe to the degree that you are afraid to compete without him or her unless you are willing to develop others to match his/her contribution.

Next, let us consider some common points in the strategic management literature that you should know sitting at the table with other persons who have a degree in business.

THREE LEVELS OF STRATEGY

Recall in Chapter 2 of Part I, we covered single- and multi-business structures. At this point, let us discuss three intentional strategies where these structures are needed:

(1) *Corporate strategy* – overarching approach used to meet long-term objectives when more than one strategic business unit exists. Prior to crafting the corporate strategy, top management (with board approval) sets the long-term direction for the company through its vision, mission, and long-term and short-term strategic objectives. A well-thought-out corporate strategy allows top management to create or exploit synergies among business units. This strategy is used by the business units to guide their strategy crafting process.

(2) *Business or competitive strategy* – approach used to meet objectives in a single business unit. Often business and competitive strategy is used

interchangeably. However, there is a difference depending on organizational structure. In companies that have only one business unit, corporate strategy, business strategy, and competitive strategy are interchangeable. In companies that have more than one unit, a business or competitive strategy (used interchangeably) is needed in each business unit to support the corporate strategy. In such cases, a vision, mission, and performance objectives should be set in each unit.

(3) *Functional strategy* – approach used to meet objectives in each functional area. Again, each area should have its own vision, mission, and performance objectives (Fig. 23).

STRATEGY TYPOLOGIES

In addition to levels of strategy, firms have been categorized by their approaches to meet performance objectives. In particular, two typologies will be discussed next. The Miles and Snow Typology of Competitive Strategy and the Astley and Fombrun Typology of Collective Strategies.

Fig. 23. Three Levels of Strategy.

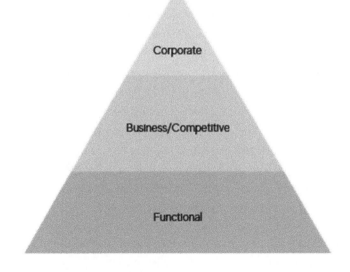

According to Raymond Miles and Charles Snow (1978/2003), four competitive strategy types are present in all industries:

1. *Defenders* – leading firms that have a hold on some products/services and markets and will use strategies to maintain their hold and protect their market share. Decision makers know the current conditions of the industry well.

2. *Prospectors* – innovators and entrepreneurial firms that seek to gain some of the hold and benefits that defenders enjoy. Using aggressive strategies, they seek to disrupt the current situation (i.e., a change in the strategic positions/market share of existing firms) and force changes in how the industry meets customer needs. New digital technologies and processes may play important roles in their strategy.

3. *Analyzers* – stable firms that are slow to change. They closely observe and analyze how defenders and prospectors respond to industry phenomena and then respond in their own best interest. Those that are slow to respond risk being caught in analysis paralysis and unable to make timely decisions.

4. *Reactors* – follower firms that are unwilling or unable to develop the kind of organizational structure that would cause other firms in an industry to consider them as a threat to their success.

Miles and Snow contend that Defenders, Analyzers, and Prospectors can be equally effective. Although the Reactor type is not considered an ideal strategy, a company may find itself in and out of this strategy at different points in the life cycle of the firm. Strategies undertaken by the key decision makers and their perception of the industry determine whether a company will be proactive or reactive. Competitors may also develop strategies based on perceptions of how well other companies are performing.

Five years later, Graham Astley and Charles Fombrun (1983) recognized the importance of firms, particularly small firms collaborating to compete and meet performance objectives. The Astley and Fombrun model categorizes firms by four collective (collaborating) strategies:

1. *Conjugate collectives* – collaborations between firms within different sectors with direct relationships (supplier–buyer).

2. *Organic collectives* – collaborations between firms from different sectors and indirect relationships (through the Small Business Administration).

3. *Confederate collectives* – collaborations between firms within the same sector with strong relationships (competitors working together).

4. *Agglomerate collectives* – collaborations between firms within the same sector with weak or indirect relationships (industry cooperation).

These competitive strategies can be used as an offensive strategy where they attempt to behave similarly to prospectors in the Miles and Snow Typology (1978/2003). Alternatively, the collectives can collaborate to defend against larger firms that have more resources. We will discuss collective strategy in Part II, Chapter 6 as a means to overcome constraints.

OBJECTIVE-BASED STRATEGIES

Like crafting pottery where the aim is to create a unique masterpiece, crafting strategies for business is done with a performance objective in mind. Objective-based strategies are intentionally crafted to be implemented. Some common intended strategies are listed in Table 9.

Three primary objectives of corporate strategies:

1. *Stabilization* – maintain the status quo based on productivity improvements.

2. *Growth* – expand the scope:

   a. New markets.

   b. New products/services.

   c. New businesses.

3. *Reorientation* – reverse declining performance:

   a. Retrenchment (belt-tightening/alignment is the objective).

   b. Turnaround (survival is the objective and a significant change in strategy is needed).

Table 9. Three Levels of Strategy.

Level	Context and Objective		Strategy
	Single business	Multiple businesses or multiple strategic business units	
Corporate		A strategy devised by the Board and Top Management that determines the direction the firm will take. Should tie all strategies together or serve as the foundation for all	Stabilization Growth Reorientation
Business/ Competitive	A strategy devised by the Board and Top Management that determines the direction the firm will take	A strategy devised by the Board and Top Management that determines the direction each business unit will take. Must align with the corporate strategy to be effective	Single business competitive Stabilization cost leadership Growth price strategy Reorientation differentiation (approaches used by both) Unmatched strengths
Functional	Strategies devised by management at various levels to determine how each functional area will support the firm's business/competitive strategy and ultimately its corporate strategy		Details that align the functional areas as needed

The objective of competitive strategy is to outperform the competition. Competitive strategy is how a company competes as a single unit or in a strategic business unit. Four common competitive strategies include:

1. *Cost Leadership* – competing based on lower cost than industry rivals (Porter, 1980).

2. *Differentiation* – competing based on perceived value or comparable worth (Porter, 1980).

3. *Unmatched Strength of a Resource* – competing based on valuable resources that are rare but demanded in an industry (includes intangible resources such as expertise, convenience, customer service, processes, etc.). This approach is also referred to as the resource-based view as these resources contribute to the advantage that one firm has over another in an industry (Barney, 1991).

4. *Price* – competing based on low price (not an ideal strategy – only makes sense when price covers cost).

Price and cost are often used interchangeably but there is a difference. Price is the amount of money or goods that a seller desires for a good or service (Fig. 24). Although a company sets the initial price, the final price or worth is the amount of money that a buyer is willing to offer, and the seller is willing to accept in an exchange transaction. Conversely, cost is the money spent to make a product or provide a service. Thus, cost is a factor in the price of a product or a service. When a product or service is exchanged for "free," or a company agrees to a price that does not reflect the perceived worth of a product or service, the cost or a portion of the worth has been absorbed by the company. This strategic approach is used often for relationship building and as an incentive to get stakeholders to try the product or service with the aim of repeat business and referrals.

Margin is the difference in cost and desired selling price. Companies operating in industries where products are easily replicated or substituted will typically have low margins. Companies that use a low cost or differentiation

---

Fig. 24.   Difference Between Cost, Price, and Worth.

Cost	Price	Worth
Money spent to make a product or provide a service	Money or goods demanded for a product or service	Money that is exchanged for a product or service.

strategy generally have high margins as they can demand more for their product or service uniqueness.

FLEXIBILITY AND EMERGENT STRATEGY

Imagine working on an assignment for months, and then one day your manager tells you to abandon your work and start something completely different without apparently considering your progress on the current assignment. Imagine this happens repeatedly. After a while, you might begin to sense that the manager does not value your work or worse, you cannot be linked to a successful strategy. The work that goes into crafting a strategy that will be considered worthy of pursuing may take time.

At any point during the strategic management process, a significant environmental change may occur and the ideas and recommendations that were initially approved may no longer be valid. Without question, companies need the flexibility to respond to changing conditions. Unplanned or unintended strategies are referred to as emergent strategies. Emergent strategies are not developed prior to strategy implementation but surface during strategy implementation. Although emergent strategies are often perceived as disruptive, they demonstrate the flexibility needed to meet objectives and therefore should intentionally be woven into the implementation plan as the need arises.

INTELLECTUAL PROPERTY

If you have a novel or an original idea, consider if your work should be protected by intellectual property (IP) laws. Know and abide by your company's IP policies, but as a thinking strategist, someone who is always thinking about how to improve things, it is possible to create something "incidental" that is outside your employer's purview. Thus, you should understand the basics of intellectual property and its commercial value and role in science, business, arts, and the professions. The Michelson 20MM Foundation provides valuable insights into this area (see https://michelsonip.com/ to learn about patents, copyrights, trademarks, and trade secrets).

FINDINGS FROM SKYE CONSTRUCTION

Recall the SMART Performance Objectives approach that was introduced earlier in this section in Chapter 4. Let us apply that approach to Skye Construction:

- *Overarching organizational goal* – Skye Construction will be a leading construction services provider in the southern part of the United States.

- *Immediate goal* – Open offices in two new states.

- *Key result area* – Revenue.

  SMART Performance Objective

- *Specific* – increase revenues – What?

- *Measurable* – by 3% (quantify performance) – How much?

- *Attainable* – yes, we have the resources needed or are committed to acquiring them – How?

- *Relevant* – yes, increasing revenues can move us closer to our vision and ultimately to our overarching organizational goal – Why?

- *Timely* – in two years (realistic deadline for achieving results) – When?

As shown in the example, performance objectives are beneficial for several reasons:

- To substitute purposeful, strategic decision making for aimless actions and confusions over what to accomplish.

- To provide a set of benchmarks for judging just how good the organization's actual strategic performance turns out to be.

- To allow for integrated thinking beyond one key result area.

While strategy does not guarantee success, managers who set objectives in key result areas are strong candidates to outperform managers who operate on hopes, prayers, and good intentions alone.

6

STRATEGIES FOR OVERCOMING CONSTRAINTS

Problem solvers must find ways to overcome constraints given they are barriers to success and limit the company's ability to gain and leverage a competitive advantage. Crafting strategy allows a company to look at multiple strategies and pursue one based on resources, and the competencies and strategic mindset of the players that will implement the strategy. A strategic mindset to overcome issues that impact performance requires assessing the situation, considering strategic options, and calculated risk-taking as part of the strategy. In Part II, Chapter 7, a number of ways to respond to risk will be identified. Whereas a risk *might* happen, a constraint is a given. A calculated risk is an outcome that has been carefully considered and determined worthy of moving forward.

Each of the following three types of strategies involves calculated risks that top management can take to address a company's constraints: no change, strategic adjustments, and synergistic development. Depending on the objective, different tactics to accomplish the strategies are shown in Table 10.

THE NO IMMEDIATE CHANGE OPTION

Sometimes the best option is not to make significant changes right now. Decision makers may decide to wait until they absolutely must change due to internal and external extremities. Some firms will make minor process changes only. Moreover, there are some advantages to being a late mover:

Table 10. Strategy Types to Overcome Restraints.

Strategies				
No Immediate Change/Active Waiting	**Strategic Adjustments**		**Synergistic Development**	
	Reduction	Strategic cost alignment	Firm growth development/ diversification	Collective strategy
	Reengineering	Selective cuts	Merger	Strategic alliance
	Restructuring	Across the board cuts	Acquisition	Joint venture
	Rightsizing	Bankruptcy	Hostile takeover	Licensing arrangement
	Divestiture			Consortium
	Liquidation			

1) Free rider (let other firms make all of the investments in research and development to fully develop a product).

2) Substitute your resources in ways that lead to a better profit.

3) Imitate a preferred strategy in hopes of being able to implement it more efficiently than the competition.

Nonetheless, there may be some dissenters who feel that not doing anything or waiting until things are "optimal" for change places the firm at a disadvantage. Developing a contingency plan that informs when a change must happen and monitoring the situation can help to assure stakeholders that action will be taken and that the company is not ignoring the possibility that change is needed. Routine updates giving everyone an opportunity to voice their concerns and providing assurances can help trigger when the contingency plan should be updated or put in place.

STRATEGIC ADJUSTMENTS

Strategic adjustments involve the day-to-day tactical improvements needed to meet objectives and achieve short-term results. They may be implemented in two forms: reductions and strategic costs alignments.

Reduction Strategies

Reduction strategies are put in place to improve performance measures such as cost, quality, customer service, and speed.

- *Reengineering* is rethinking and redesigning business processes, primarily to eliminate unnecessary activities or improve activities that are underperforming.

- *Restructuring* is changing the structure of the organization to improve performance, primarily through a simpler decision making structure.

- *Rightsizing* is any kind of reduction in the workforce. Often used when the number of employees exceeds the number needed for efficient delivery of products or services.

- *Divestiture* is selling subsidiary business interests or investments to another firm. The firm will exist but under new ownership.

- *Liquidation* is closing down a subsidiary's business interests or investments. This is not the same as a liquidation sale where inventory is sold. The firm will cease to exist.

STRATEGIC COST ALIGNMENT

A good place to start to determine if a change is needed is to determine if the firm's costs and prices are competitive. Fixed costs are costs that are independent of output. They remain constant over a period of time and include rent, buildings, machinery, etc. Alternatively, variable costs are costs that vary with output. Generally, variable costs increase at a constant rate relative to labor and capital. Variable costs may include wages, utilities, materials used in production, hours in service delivery, etc. Mixed costs are part fixed and part variable and include electricity, phone and Internet usage, overtime pay, etc.

One of the first steps to smarter, more strategic cost cutting is gaining an understanding of the differences among budget, cost, price, subsidy/discount, and revenue as shown in Fig. 25.

Bad costs, good costs, and best costs exist as shown in Fig. 26.

Fig. 25.   Money in the Strategic Money Process.

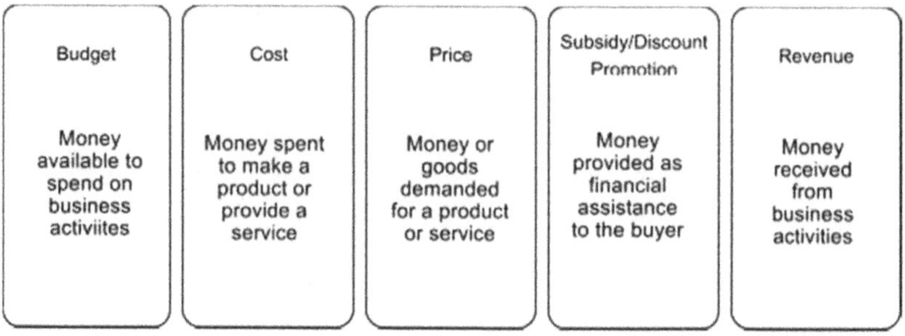

Budget	Cost	Price	Subsidy/Discount Promotion	Revenue
Money available to spend on business activiites	Money spent to make a product or provide a service	Money or goods demanded for a product or service	Money provided as financial assistance to the buyer	Money received from business activities

Let us start with bad costs. Bad costs are unwanted costs that managers seek to avoid and eliminate due to constraints and operational inefficiencies. Bad industry costs (the cost of doing business in an industry) should be minimized by internal processes. Good costs are simply the cost of pursuing a particular strategy in line with others in the industry. Lastly, best costs are

Fig. 26.   Bad Costs, Good Cost, and Best Costs.

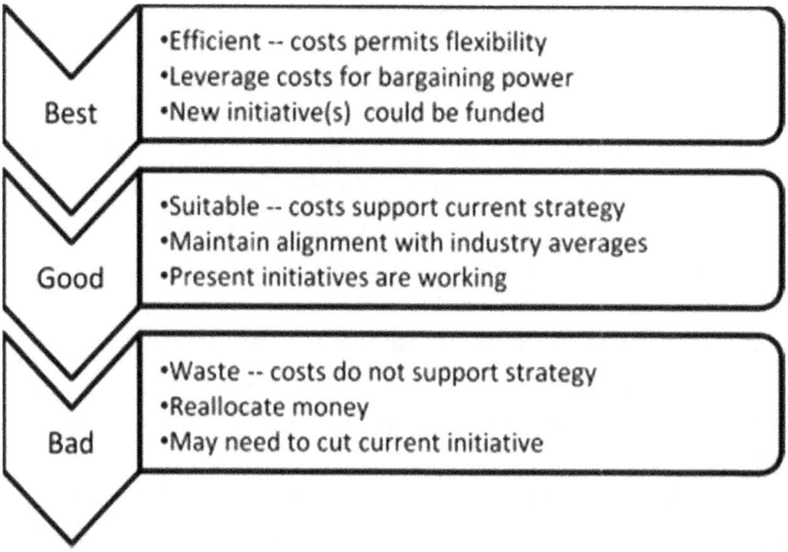

Best
•Efficient -- costs permits flexibility
•Leverage costs for bargaining power
•New initiative(s) could be funded

Good
•Suitable -- costs support current strategy
•Maintain alignment with industry averages
•Present initiatives are working

Bad
•Waste -- costs do not support strategy
•Reallocate money
•May need to cut current initiative

costs that enable the firm to leverage its collective strengths to gain a competitive advantage. Best costs may lead to a low cost strategy or a differentiated strategy where buyers see value in the production process.

Selective Versus Across-The-Board Cuts. In selective cost cutting, problem solvers look at each activity in the cost structure to determine where bad cost exists and seek to cut those costs. Moreover, they attempt to find ways to improve good costs where possible. Conversely, across the board cuts do not consider if the costs are bad, good, or best. In across-the-board cost cutting, problem solvers cut costs throughout the cost structure. For example, if the decision makers determine a 15% reduction in cost across the board is needed – every budget would be cut 15%.

Note that selective cuts that only look at performance may be detrimental. There may be some rising stars in the mix that are not in the top quartile and cutting those initiatives may not be the best option. Moreover, there may be a top performer that is expected to see a downturn in activity. Selective cuts require thought beyond basic criteria.

Bankruptcy. A company that is experiencing financial hardship may opt to file bankruptcy under bankruptcy laws. Two options exist – either dissolve or reorganize.

- Dissolve (liquidate assets) – Chapter 7.

- Reorganize (adjustments of debt to save the firm and pay back creditors according to a repayment plan while finding a more profitable way of doing business) – Chapter 11 and (adjustment for a family farmer or fisherman) – Chapter 12.

Not all debts are dischargeable. The Bankruptcy Code lists categories of debt excepted from discharge under Chapters 7, 11, and 12. If the court decides the plan is workable, the plan is sent to all creditors listed for review. An objection to the discharge may be filed by a creditor, by the trustee in the case, or by the US trustee. A bankruptcy court will decide the matter.

Reduction strategies help a company compete better. Additionally, by reining in costs, a firm becomes more attractive to stakeholders. Prices can be lowered to attract more price-sensitive buyers. Creditors are willing to lend more for projects. Opportunities to partner with complementors and other firms become more enticing to both parties.

Stakeholders will certainly be impacted by any of the reduction strategies. All may eliminate jobs and create the need for job redesigns to ensure that the work can be done with less. Announcements should happen early and updates often and should include efforts to assist affected individuals, departments, strategic business units, and external stakeholders as they adjust to the needed changes. Moreover, it is important to acknowledge the "new normal" when things stabilize.

SYNERGISTIC DEVELOPMENT

Synergistic development is a strategy between two firms. According to Goold and Campbell (1998) synergy can be demonstrating in six ways:

1. benefiting from knowledge and skills;

2. coordinated strategies;

3. shared tangible resources;

4. economies of scale;

5. gaining bargaining power over suppliers; and

6. creating new products or services.

Synergistic development implies that the collective strength of a company is not adequate to accomplish the goals set by the board and top management. The advantages of synergistic development include working with different partners (buyers, suppliers, competitors, complementors, government agencies, etc.) in order to compete for opportunities primarily through sharing project costs, and pooling resources to manage risks.

FIRM GROWTH/DIVERSIFICATION

A company can overcome constraints by targeting another company for growth and development when it is deemed that the combined strength of the two companies can lead to a competitive advantage (1 + 1=3).

Diversification can be accomplished through any of the following:

(1) *Merger* – the combining of operations of two or more often similarly sized-collaborative companies with the approval of the board and top management of both companies:

- *Horizontal merger*: both companies operate in the same industry and are competitors in the same market.

- *Vertical merger*: firms that operate in different production or delivery stages of the same industry.

- *Conglomerate merger*: two or more companies belonging to different industrial sectors combine their operations.

(2) *Acquisition* – a purchase of one company by another company with the approval of the board and top management of both companies. These companies are often not similarly sized with the larger company acquiring the smaller company.

(3) *Hostile takeover* – the results of efforts of the board and top management of a company that has targeted another company for a merger or acquisition, but the target company's board or top management is unwilling to approve the merger or acquisition.

In all cases, there is an expectation of above average shareholder returns as a result of these strategies. In some cases, when there is a presumed imbalance of power in an industry as a result of these strategies, the government may prohibit these actions from going forward. In all successful cases, there is a dissolution of one of the firms or a restructuring to allow for a new strategy and the expected increase in performance. Thus, the decision makers must consider whether to enter new industries that are related or unrelated to their current business ventures.

As noted by theorists Gamble, Thompson, and Peteraf (2013), firms can enhance shareholder value by diversifying into related businesses given the skills and capabilities, facilities, and other resources that can be transferred from one company to the other. They also note that by diversifying into unrelated business(es), firms can spread their risk across other types of businesses or markets.

COLLECTIVE STRATEGY

Cooperating with other companies is a means of pooling resources to achieve competitive parity. Companies can work collectively through the following strategies:

- *Strategic Alliance* – agreement between or among firms (usually short term) to pursue a set of agreed-upon objectives needed while remaining independent organizations.

- *Joint Venture* – agreement in which the parties agree to develop a new business entity by contributing equity.

- *Licensing Arrangement* – agreement to produce or sell a product owned by the licensor.

- *Consortium* – agreement among similar firms to pool resources for greater efficiencies.

- *Value Chain* – agreement between suppliers and buyers for greater efficiencies as well as market expansion.

PARTNERING OR DOING BUSINESS WITH MINORITY BUSINESS ENTERPRISES

Business collaborations with minority business enterprises (MBEs), also referred to as minority-owned businesses, have been shown to be a viable option for firms (Edmondson & Munchus, 2001). In MBEs, 51% of the owners (privately held) or shares (publicly held) are held by Blacks, Asians, Hispanics, and or Native Americans (see http://www.nmsdc.org/mbes/what-is-an-mbe/). MBEs are often small and medium-sized for-profit firms with historically documented capacity constraints. They often collaborate with external partners to grow and compete successfully. The US federal government has assisted the development of MBEs by using its power as a large buyer to compel the business sector to help implement a variety of social and economic policies.

Three executive orders were put in place to regulate these partnerships. Executive Order 109255 (1962) requires companies with or seeking contracts with the federal government to use affirmative action to ensure that minority and female workers are considered for all jobs. Executive Order 11458 (March 5, 1969) stipulated government agencies and their contractors should partner up with minority-owned companies. As a result, some major companies partner with MBEs to get incentives offered by the government. To prevent fraud and illegal opportunistic behavior, Executive Order 11625 (signed Oct. 13, 1971) was put into place to define an MBE. The Order stipulated that MBEs are business enterprises that are owned or controlled by one or more socially or economically disadvantaged persons. Such disadvantages may arise from cultural, racial, chronic economic circumstances or background or similar cases.

Competitive strategy models that include MBEs firms can lead to improved performance. However, firms have complained that they are unable to find businesses owned by people of color. Thus, The National Minority Supplier Development Council and state-run Minority Supplier Development Councils certify businesses owned by people of color as MBEs based on established criteria which include a combination of screenings, interviews, and site visits. The councils connect and promote relationships between majority corporate members with MBEs and relationships among MBEs.

Prior to making these connections, it is important to consider the different strategy types of MBEs. Edmondson (1996) identified five strategy types of minority enterprises along five dimensions:

- The aim or objective of the business owners.

- Key relationships the firm has with other players in the industry.

- Kinds of business opportunities pursued.

- Owners' attitude toward risk.

- Capital and access to credit.

As shown in Table 11, MBE strategy types include the following:

- *Anchors* distinguish their firms by gaining a clear understanding of the needs of the community they serve and may be willing to offer a service that non-minority firms are unwilling or unable to offer. Anchors in pursuit of government contracts are competent and know where to go for assistance.

Table 11. Five Strategy Types for MBEs.

Dimensions	Strategy Types				
	Anchors	Adventurers	Adaptors	Amplers	Amateurs
Aim or Objectives	Profit/ Growth	Profit/ Growth	Profit/ Growth	Profit/ Growth	Autonomy/ Survival
Key Relationships	Buyer– Supplier	Competitor– Competitor	Buyer–Supplier Competitor– Competitor	Buyer- Supplier	Competitor- Customer
Opportunities Pursued	Narrow Markets	Unrelated to Core Business	Related to Core Business	Related to Core Business	Skilled Based
Attitude Toward Risk	Averse	Takers	Averse	Averse	Takers
Capital and Access to Credit	Limited	Limited	Limited	Sufficient	Limited

- *Adventurers* actively seek new opportunities that may not be closely related to their core business or within their community. They are willing to link to one another to strengthen their capabilities. Adventurers in pursuit of government contracts are also competent and know where to go for assistance.

- *Adaptors* are managed or owned by persons who like the stability of working with a select few buyers or suppliers and are sometimes willing to take risks that are closely tied to their core business. They may compete against a company on one project and team up with the same competitor on another. Like Anchors and Adventurers, Adaptors in pursuit of government contracts are competent and know where to go for assistance.

- *Amplers* were initially thought to be amateurs with very little business acumen. However, the research showed that these firms are far from amateurs. They are in business because they want to control their own destiny-they want to be their own bosses or not work in corporate America which is often viewed by people of color as being controlled by the dominant culture. Survival of the firm will be a key objective and they are likely to pursue opportunities when they have skill. Some will market themselves as "jacks of all trades" capable of handling work in a general area. They are not likely to pursue government contracts.

- *Amateurs* are in business because they want to control their own destinies, they want to be their own bosses, and survival of the firm will a key objective. While they know what the competition is doing, they make little if any attempt to distinguish themselves from their competitors. Instead, they focus on satisfying the needs of their customers. Within the strategy types, they are viewed as having little business acumen.

Not only has the federal government sought to help firms owned by people of color, but in 2000, Executive Order 13157 was put in place to provide similar opportunities for women-owned small businesses. Reaching out to firms owned by people of color and women for partnerships can open up doors.

BUILDING LINKS WITH BUSINESS SCHOOLS

The firm's intellectual capital can be enhanced by students who serve as interns, (whose time is less expensive) or on a team of consultants in a project-based learning experience (whose services are free). Depending on your company's needs, the faculty's course learning objectives, and the students' interests and skills, your company can benefit from the fresh perspectives of students about your strategies. These experiences provide contextual insights that help students get a glimpse into some of the challenges facing decision makers. Moreover, the outcome of these experiences helps institutions assess the rigor and relevance of their academic program.

As noted by Edmondson, Zebal, Bhuiyan, Crumbly, and Jackson (2021), students can pursue their passion, develop their skill sets and prepare for their careers beyond graduation. While interns can learn about the routine and time-consuming activities that everyone must know to be successful in the field, to really take advantage of having select students in place, encourage them to speak up in meetings and brainstorming sessions, assign them to work on a project under the supervision of a problem solver who can mentor the student as well as gain additional knowledge and expertise, and require them to prepare and participate in presentations. Additionally, project-based learning provides teams of students under the direction of a faculty member with in-depth real-time experience that cannot be learned from reading cases. Again, engaging a problem solver who can provide insights into an issue the company is facing is essential. Moreover, contributors from the firm should be prepared to share financials and other confidential information to the team of student consultants as well as be available to attend and participate in one or more presentations to their class.

Whether these experiences are onsite-based or conducted remotely or virtually, for academic credit, they must be a learning experience that allows students to apply the knowledge gained in the classroom. It must not be used as a chance to outsource routine work that a regular employee would perform. By hosting an orientation prior to selecting interns and agreeing to participate in a consulting project, your company can communicate expectations and answer questions that students and faculty may have to achieve better results. For example, if an institution has stipulated a minimum number of working/client interfacing hours for academic credit, it is best to know that prior to the start of the selection process (especially if you seek to work with students from more than one institution) and before making the commitment to work with the consulting team. When an internship is not for academic credit, the company has control over how to conduct the experience and whether it is paid or unpaid, thus communicating the expectations early enables both sides to make informed decisions.

The more resources your company is willing to put toward links with business schools (or other areas where expertise is needed), the more it will be able to attract great students. Both internships and project-based learning teams are great networking and recruitment opportunities as companies often seek to retain the students with potential for entry-level hires.

CAVEATS

While synergistic development may appear to be a quick fix, it inherently brings along risks and costs when things do not go as planned. Thus, choosing a partner and monitoring activities is essential. Although Coras, Tantau, and Dumitrum (2013) make a good case for open innovation projects based on trust, partnering with a firm that you directly compete with can be problematic. Therefore, I argue that a contract outlining expectations and consequences for failing to meet those expectations are imperative. Additionally, leaders may be challenged in getting people to move beyond differences in cultures and processes in order to benefit from the expected shared knowledge and expertise that would ultimately lead to profits.

Constraints can limit a company's choices; however, they can also open the company up to new opportunities and induce the decision makers to be creative in their business models. It is important to include voices from all significantly impacted stakeholder groups to determine the new strategy that will guide their decision making process. For optimal results, these discussions should take place prior to contract signings. However, note that once the developments are in place, additional concerns may surface or something that was assumed to be an issue does not surface. Issues that are not resolved can derail the agreement; thus, it is essential to anticipate and address them in real time.

For Your Tool

Think about other areas that you use strategy. What makes you a strategic thinker in those areas? How were you able to relate some of the content in this chapter with how you currently strategize? What elements found in this chapter can you adapt to become a better strategist using what you already do well.

7

COLLABORATIVE DECISION MAKING

Given the vast options that are available to resolve a strategic issue, a team of decision makers may find the task daunting. Members come to a decision in various ways: intuition, past performance, research, books, videos, experience, etc. A structured collaborative decision making process can make the process run smoothly and ensure there is a strategic fit between what is proposed and what has already been decided. While dissent should be welcomed in the process, at some point the decision makers must come to an agreement. Doing so increases the likelihood that problem solvers and contributors have a better idea of the activities they should do to bring about the change the decision makers want to see. The need for agreement during the strategic management process cannot be overemphasized (Fig. 27).

BRAINWRITING

Before you go to a brainstorming session, using the agenda as your guide, take time to think about the topics that are likely to be discussed. Write down your perspectives about each topic. If a topic is on the agenda that you are not familiar with, then research the topic to get different perspectives. Look for previous internal communications about these topics. If you find articles written about the topic on the internet or in databases, in addition to recording what was recommended, note the credentials of the "experts" of whose opinion you find relevant in either supporting or refuting your view. Were their opinions applicable to all industries, specific industries, and to your

---

Fig. 27. The Need for Agreement.

collaboration

contibution agreement

---

company or job function in particular? Refer to this list and add to it during the brainstorming session. This act will demonstrate that you have carefully considered your input and it is supported by credentialed others within your firm and in the field.

BRAINSTORMING

We have discussed brainstorming throughout this text. Brainstorming has become a buzzword for anytime a group of problem solvers meet to discuss an issue. This engaging process is not a problem-solving analysis, but a communication tool that is used across most analyses. As shown in the collaborative decision making model (Fig. 28), brainstorming is used to identify the top options that meet stakeholder needs. All key players in a transaction are expected to inform the decision by providing insights to the group and the facilitator that might otherwise go unreported. However, once the key decision makers agree on what needs to change and why, the participants are expected to gather relevant information to learn about the options and implications of each. If you have participated in a brainstorming session, you may realize just how important the second step is to the success of the process. Refer back to Chapter 1 of Part II on how to gather the information.

At this point, let us turn to how to ensure that the top options are discussed and expose some of the barriers that may negatively impact the experience. Below are eight barriers that can surface in the session:

Fig. 28. Collaborative Decision Making Process.

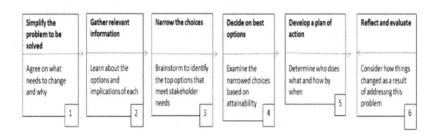

1. *One Right Answer Syndrome.* If you believe that there is only one way to handle a specific problem, you will be prone to close your mind to other approaches.

2. *Fear of Failure.* If you have not had success in recent implementations, that fear could cloud how you view the current opportunity.

3. *Self-interest.* If you are concerned about protecting your own function rather than looking out for the best interests of the company, that mindset could be disastrous especially if more than one participant shares the same mindset or if no one is willing to acknowledge when self-interest is an issue in the session.

4. *Experience, Vested Interest in the Status Quo.* If you've done things one way for a while and have had some success doing that way, you might think that way is the best way to do things in the future.

5. *Training, Education.* If you were taught to do something one way, you might be risk-averse and perceive change as unnecessary or too costly.

6. *Assumptions.* If you make assumptions rather than asking for clarity, those assumptions could direct your thinking in a particular direction.

7. *Judgments.* If you make up your mind about an option before hearing the pros and cons, those judgments keep you from being objective. When expressed to the group, they often shut down the discussion on that option.

8. *Thinking Patterns.* If you fail to consider that not everyone at the table has the same level of knowledge, experience, or intelligence, then you may not give each person enough time or information to come to a decision. Those who "get it" or understand how the option can work should point out the factors that matter so that those who need help understanding get to a point where they feel comfortable making a decision.

AGREEMENT ON THE IMPORTANT ISSUES

The key decision makers will determine who should be involved in each step of the decision making process. Therefore, different players may be included in each step. Thus, communicating agreed expectations helps to keep problem solvers and contributors on the right track and helps to resolve internal group conflicts. For example, if top management has determined that an increase in sales is something that it wants to accomplish, having a reduction in the sales force does not appear to be going in the right direction. A problem solver should question whether this tactic is suitable for implementation.

When crafting strategies, it is important to agree on some expectations early in the process. Agree on:

- the problem to be solved;

- the ideal option;

- the key result areas;

- the method(s) to analyze the situation;

- the desired outcomes for each key result area;

- quantitative performance expectations; and

- risk management and contingencies.

Agreement does not mean unanimity of thought as indicated by a unanimous vote or no dissenting opinions. It means that the team consents to a set of parameters that will ensure that progress can be made. Reflecting and evaluating a step may lead to the need to go back and develop another plan of action.

Agree on the Problem to be Solved

Lest the decision makers believe the company has enough resources to address multiple problems simultaneously, prioritizing problems is essential. Priority should be based on importance, urgency, and attainability:

1. After brainstorming to identify the problems that are perceived to be important to meeting performance objectives, the decision makers should identify and rank the top three or more.

2. Additionally, in a separate listing, identify and rank urgent matters – those things that should be given close attention based on deadlines.

3. Compare and contrast the two lists and make a third list based on the rankings of both. Problems that appear on both lists will be used to determine which problem(s) are given more consideration.

4. The next step is to determine if the organization can successfully address the problem with current resources, and if not, are the decision makers willing to secure the resources needed. The result of this process may reveal that the company can address multiple problems simultaneously. The final step is to hold meetings with problem solvers to paint a clear picture of the problem(s) to be solved and to disclose why management decided to solve this problem(s) and not others.

Agree on the Ideal Option

Picturing the best-case scenario enables problem solvers to envision how conditions would be if resources were not limited. Think of it as a job description where the human resources professional lists out the responsibilities of the candidate. Included in the job description are the qualifications outlining the preferred educational background and work experience that would be ideal for the role that the company wants to fill. Using this proactive approach not only allows the decision makers to determine when an option is well suited to solve the problem, but it also allows them to quickly eliminate an option that does not compare well to the ideal option.

Agree on Key Result Areas

Result areas help to determine where attention will be placed in the process. Again, lest the decision makers deemed they have unlimited resources to tackle one or more problems, narrowing down the number of areas helps to improve the likelihood of success in those key areas. The number of key result areas depends on the resources available that allow close attention to detail. At this point, metrics are not set. Instead, the decision makers understand that metrics must be determined.

Agree on Method(s) That Will Be Used to Analyze the Situation

Three common approaches to anticipate changes in the environment when deciding on strategic options are:

1. *Forecasting* – consider resources and constraints based on hindsight and how they affected past performance on financial stations.

2. *Predicting* – consider resources and constraints based on developments since the last performance cycle and future expectations on pro forma statements.

3. *Scenario Planning* – consider resources and constraints based on what ifs to determine how your stakeholders might respond.

There is an abundance of forecasting tools available. Forecasting is most helpful when no significant changes are expected. The problem solver can use historical data in the tool and anticipate outcomes with some confidence. Conversely, when significant changes are expected, the problem solver should not rely solely on past data. Adjustments should be made based on additional research that can inform the decision makers about how those changes are likely to impact the organization. Confidence in outcomes is based on the quality of information available about the anticipated changes.

Agree on Desired Outcomes for Each Key Result Area

After the key result areas are determined, the decision makers must agree on the desired outcomes they would like to see in each area and how those outcomes impact system effectiveness. What quality standards will meet their expectations?

Agree on Quantitative Performance Expectations

Once there is an agreement on system effectiveness within the key areas, the decision makers can now quantify their expectations. Ranges for each of the categories below are needed beginning with 0 as a possibility indicating the worst situation and 10 as the ultimate situation (Fig. 29):

- Satisfactory

- Sufficient

- Unsatisfactory

- Unacceptable

Fig. 29.   Satisfaction Ranges.

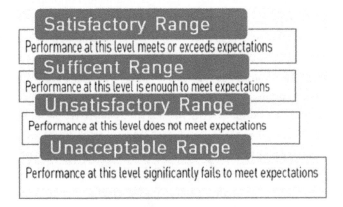

Satisfactory Range
Performance at this level meets or exceeds expectations

Sufficent Range
Performance at this level is enough to meet expectations

Unsatisfactory Range
Performance at this level does not meet expectations

Unacceptable Range
Performance at this level significantly fails to meet expectations

Agree on Risk Management and Contingencies

What could change? Part of the strategy making process is simply acknowledging that mistakes can be made when crafting strategies, that something can change, or that something can go wrong and that there are implications when either of these situations exists. Even under the best circumstances, when everyone agrees- there are no guarantees in strategy. More on risk management in Part II, Chapter 8.

DECISION ANALYSIS

Carefully consider the resources and constraints that were identified in the environmental analyses. The output of those analyses is the input for crafting strategy and decision analysis. To overcome some of the barriers listed above, a decision analysis can be useful in deciding on the best option. A decision analysis has eight steps:

Step 1 is reframing the problem into a decision statement that reflects what the key decision makers would like to accomplish-the change they would like to see or the objective. The statement should reflect that the company intends to find the best or optimal solution.

Step 2 is engaging in further discussions with key decision makers to establish a set of strategy-based objectives.

Step 3 is weighing each of the objectives established in Step 2 to establish their importance in influencing the outcome of the decision and actual performance. Given every objective was suggested by someone in a key role; each objective should be ranked in descending order by criteria set by management. Once the ranks are completed, weights of importance ranging from 10 (very high important; mandatory) to 1 (not important; optional) are assigned. Every objective should not be valued as "very important"; thus, each objective should be weighted compared to the other criteria. Only objectives with a value of ≥5 are significant and should be recommended to the management team. If it is later determined that an objective was left out of the analysis because it was incorrectly weighted, then reassign a weight greater than or equal to 5 and gain an understanding of why this error occurred. The number of objectives in the analysis is not a constraint. The number of objectives should be determined based on what can realistically be attained.

Step 4 is determining the satisfaction ranges that will be used as part of a satisfaction scale for the strategy-based objectives. The best option(s) should align well with the selected objectives. Satisfaction ranges are used by decision makers to evaluate how well each objective has been met by an option under consideration. The high end of the range is 10 and the low end is 0. Quantified ranges make it easier to score options as they remove subjectivity. For example, "100 sales calls = 10" is easier to assess than "high number of sales calls =10."

It is not necessary to assign a value to each number between 10 and 0, but it is recommended that a range for each of the following levels is set: Satisfactory, Sufficient, Unsatisfactory, and Unacceptable. However, until you become proficient at assigning scores (Step 6), it is a good idea to develop ranges for all numbers between 10 and 0 and keep those ranges in an Appendix. The values for the levels may differ from analysis to analysis; however, within the analysis of the same strategic issue the values should be consistent for uniformity. When meeting with the decision makers to discuss the process or outcomes (Step 8), you can present only the ranges for the suggested four levels. However, if the decision makers prefer to see/discuss the ranges for all 11 numbers (0–10), then by all means follow their lead.

Step 5 is generating a list of the strategic options that can meet the objectives based on objectives-based research. Prior to delving into the decision matrix, it is a good idea to explore each option and explain why it was included in the analysis. Visuals are better than narratives at painting a picture of what can be done. Discussing each option's attainability based on internal and external analyses ensures that realistic strategies are under consideration. At least one strategic option should be perceived as a 10 for each objective in the analysis.

Step 6 is researching each strategic option to derive a score for each based on the objectives.

Any score between 10 and 0 may be assigned to each option. Don't limit yourself to the values within the satisfaction ranges. Allow for proximity within ranges as some options may score a 9 on a 10–7–4–0 satisfaction scale (close to the ultimate situation) or a 7 on a 10–5–0 satisfaction scale (better than the average situation).

Step 7 is developing a matrix that will allow you to compare and choose the best option(s). Best practice is to confirm objectives, weights, satisfaction ranges, and options with key decision makers prior to moving ahead with the next step but certainly before this step. As you consider all the options, take notes of potential problems that can arise if you choose each one as you work through the plan. Potential problems and their likely causes will be addressed as part of implementation planning.

Step 8 is presenting a draft of the Decision Matrix (prior to the analysis) and the Decision Analysis to the decision makers for input and commitment. Discuss the impractical options first showing why they will not work and mention that they were considered and have been/ will be included in an Appendix. Then, discuss the practical solutions that will be/were covered in the decision analysis. Answer questions, resolve conflict, remove inaccuracies, build consensus, and adjust as necessary before implementation planning begins. Be prepared to make changes to your spreadsheets and presentation software in real time. Follow-up within 24 hrs. Meet with the decision makers as a whole or individually as often as necessary for clarity and direction when you are not able to move forward without additional input beyond your research findings.

DECISION MODES

William Altier (1999) recommended using one of three decision modes to direct the analysis: select, determine, or develop. In the select mode, one mutually exclusive strategic option is chosen, and all others are eliminated. This mode is best when the decision makers plan to identify only one strategic option (the best one). In the determine mode, there is a perception that the best option may be a combination of two options that are not mutually exclusive, and each option together would be better than separately. In the develop mode, there is no known viable and attainable option(s) that meet the mandatory objectives from which to choose, and thus at least one viable and attainable option must be developed by the problem solvers. Note, it may not be optimal, but it should help the firm meet its objectives and may be further developed later.

Whether someone uses the select or determine mode is based on expectations at the time the analysis begins. The idea of options being mutually exclusive is simple when the aim is choosing one or more products or services over another. However, strategy is a set of activities and when you are identifying a strategy – you are looking for a combination of activities that will work. Thus, based on the results and changes in perceived attainability, an analysis that was expected to have only one solution may result in two solutions. Moreover, an analysis that was expected to have more than one solution may result in only one. This outcome does not automatically assume that a misjudgment was made at the onset of the analysis and therefore the results cannot be used. Instead, it highlights that the need to be flexible in the analysis far outweighs the need to be right at the start. The reason for the change should be evident based on the research. Likewise, when the problem solvers are unable to present an adequate number of options (including in the development mode) it reduces the number of options the company has to consider. There should be agreement on the number of options under consideration at the beginning of the analysis. Moreover, include all options and associated data in an Appendix in case someone wants to know if other objectives or options were considered allowing stakeholders and you to refer to it for additional information and insights.

For minor decisions, it may seem like overkill to use decision analysis, include an Appendix, etc. However, the experience you gain from using the process on small matters will serve you well when you must work on complex matters. Next, let us explore how addressing the strategic issues discussed in a CRT can aid in the decision making process in Skye Construction.

FINDINGS FROM SKYE CONSTRUCTION

The Current Reality Tree revealed that Skye Construction is experiencing a decline in revenue as evidenced by a decrease in productivity and unstable sales growth. The next step is to determine how best to address the constraints to reverse the decline in revenue.

The task force used Decision Analysis to identify the best option to address the strategic issue. Based on their brainstorming session, they agreed to use the determine mode because they sensed that more than one option was suitable. As a result of the task force's thorough decision analysis, Skye Construction was able to determine which strategic options would have the best impact on the future performance of the firm. The results of their analysis follow.

As shown in Tables 12–19, after writing a succinct statement that guided their analysis, they established strategy-based objectives that correlated with the CEO's immediate goal to increase revenue. Each objective was assigned a weight based on its relative influence on the final decision according to discussions with key decision makers across the company, as well as the C-suite. For this analysis, as shown in Table 12, the CEO determined that objectives that were assigned a weight between 10 and 5 are considered important enough to warrant further consideration in the analysis.

As shown in Table 13, the task force eliminated objectives with weights less than 7. Those objectives will be included in an Appendix.

As shown in Table 14, satisfaction ranges were developed for each objective that remained in the analysis to determine how well an option satisfies that objective. The satisfaction ranges for Skye Construction are below. The

Table 12. Weighting Objectives.

Current Reality: Skye Construction is experiencing a decline in revenue as evidenced by a decrease in productivity and unstable sales growth

Decision Analysis Statement: Determine the best approach to reverse declining revenues

Strategy-based objectives	Weight
Maximize profit	10
Improve workplace environment	10
Maximize relationships strategic partners	9
Differentiate products and services from competitors	9
Maximize the utilization of the current capabilities	8
Maximize social media presence	7

Table 13. Appendix of Eliminated Objectives

Current Reality: Skye Construction is experiencing a decline in revenue as evidenced by a decrease in productivity and unstable sales growth
Decision Analysis Statement: Determine the best approach to reverse declining revenues

ELIMINATED OBJECTIVES	
Increase customer contact	6
Increase partnerships with Black-owned companies	5
Increase visibility of the Foundation	4

team chose 10 = Satisfactory, 7 = Sufficient, 4 = Unsatisfactory, and 0 = Unacceptable as standard measures. Recall that these numbers are not the only scores that can be assigned to a strategic option.

After the satisfaction ranges for each objective had been established, the team met to reconsider the CRT, and to brainstorm and agree on the strategic options that would be included in the analysis. Table 15 is the matrix that captures the strategy-based objectives and their weights along with the strategic options. Across the top of the matrix is the objective not met identified in the Current Reality Tree and the Decision Analysis Statement. The first column on the left is the list of strategy-based objectives in order of their corresponding weighted importance. The letters A–D represent the different strategic options identified as represented in the legend below. Each option's letter has two columns, one for its score and one for its weighted score. There are two additional rows – one for the total weighted scores for each strategic option and one for the final decision.

Each option was researched with the strategy-based objectives in mind and given a score based on the satisfaction ranges. Table 16 shows the score for each objective based on the satisfaction ranges. For example, decision makers rated option B (partner with complementors) as a 7 (satisfactory) to achieve the "Maximize profit" objective because this option was deemed to meet the industry average on costs. Again, notice that scores other than 10, 7, 4, and 0 are assigned when the scores for the options fall between the ranges.

Table 17 shows the weighted scores when each option was multiplied by the weight of the objective.

Table 14.   Skye Construction Satisfaction Scale.

Current Reality: Skye Construction is experiencing a decline in revenue as evidenced by a decrease in productivity and unstable sales growth
Decision Analysis Statement: Determine the best approach to reverse declining revenues

Strategy-based Objectives with Weights

Maximize profit = 10

Effectively controlled costs	10
Meet industry average on costs	7
Achieve break even sales volume	4
Merely use a low-price strategy to cover cost	0

Improve workplace environment = 10

Shifts company culture	10
Will enhance the workplace environment	7
Will cause some change in the workplace environment	4
Will have minimal impact on the workplace environment	0

Maximize relationships strategic partners = 9

Significantly enhances relationship with strategic partners	10
Little positive impact on relationships with strategic partners	7
Will not impact relationship with strategic partners	4
Negatively impacts relationships with strategic partners	0

Differentiate products and services from competitors = 9

Provide options that competitors do not offer	10
Provide new similar options	7
Provide new identical options of competitors	4
Maintain same options	0

Maximize the utilization of the current capabilities = 8

Best use of current capabilities	10
Minor deficiencies are tolerable	7
Deficiencies will need to be addressed	4
Exposes too many constraints in current processes	0

Maximize social media presence = 7

Increase by 26% in total followers all accounts	10
Increase by 25% to 20% in total followers all accounts	7
Increase by 19% to 16% in total followers all accounts	4
Increase by <15% in total followers all accounts	0

Table 15.   Decision Matrix 1.

Current Reality: Skye Construction is experiencing a decline in revenue as evidenced by a decrease in productivity and unstable sales growth
Decision Analysis Statement: Determine the best approach to reverse declining revenues

Strategy-based Objectives	WT	A SC	WT SC	B SC	WT SC	C SC	WT SC	D SC	WT SC
1. Maximize profit	10								
2. Improve workplace environment	10								
3. Maximize relationships strategic partners	9								
4. Differentiate products and services from competitors	9								
5. Maximize the utilization of the current capabilities	8								
6. Maximize social media presence	7								
Total weighted scores									

Final decision:

Strategic Options Legend:
A = Reduce amount of time to complete projects (differentiation strategy)
B = Partner with complementors
C = Improve branding
D = Find cheaper materials (cost leadership strategy)

Table 18 shows the analysis with all weighted scores added together for each option. Note that in this analysis, the final weighted scores are relatively close, indicating the strategic options were considered to be viable options and the research did not show grave differences in outcomes. In some cases, there may be a clear winner where there is a strategic option with a weighted score that is significantly higher than the others. In some cases, there may be clear underdogs where there are one or more strategic options with a weighted score that is significantly lower than others. In cases such as this,

Table 16.   Decision Matrix 2.

Current Reality: Skye Construction is experiencing a decline in revenue as evidenced by a decrease in productivity and unstable sales growth
Decision Analysis Statement: Determine the best approach to reverse declining revenues

Strategy-based Objectives	WT	**A** SC	WT SC	**B** SC	WT SC	**C** SC	WT SC	**D** SC	WT SC
1. Maximize profit	10	10		7		7		9	
2. Improve workplace environment	10	2		2		8		5	
3. Maximize relationships strategic partners	9	10		10		7		10	
4. Differentiate products and services from competitors	9	7		5		10		4	
5. Maximize the utilization of the current capabilities	8	4		10		0		10	
6. Maximize social media presence	7	7		8		9		0	
Total weighted scores									

Final decision:

Strategic Options Legend:
A = Reduce amount of time to complete projects (differentiation strategy)
B = Partner with complementors
C = Improve branding
D = Find cheaper materials (cost leadership strategy)

where no clear winner exists, the decision makers may opt to go with an option that did not receive the highest weighted score. Again, flexibility is a difference maker, and it is important not to limit what the firm does based solely on the decision analysis in these cases.

Table 17. Decision Matrix 3.

Current Reality: Skye Construction is experiencing a decline in revenue as evidenced by a decrease in productivity and unstable sales growth
Decision Analysis Statement: Determine the best approach to reverse declining revenues

		A		B		C		D	
Strategy-based Objectives	WT	SC	**WT SC**	SC	**WT SC**	SC	**WT SC**	SC	**WT SC**
1. Maximize profit	10	10	100	7	70	7	70	9	90
2. Improve workplace environment	10	3	30	2	20	8	80	5	50
3. Maximize relationships strategic partners	9	10	90	10	90	7	63	10	90
4. Differentiate products and services from competitors	9	7	63	5	45	10	90	4	36
5. Maximize the utilization of the current capabilities	8	4	32	10	80	0	0	10	80
6. Maximize social media presence	7	7	49	8	56	9	63	0	0
Total weighted scores									

Final decision:

Strategic Options Legend:
A = Reduce amount of time to complete projects (differentiation strategy)
B = Partner with complementors
C = Improve branding
D = Find cheaper materials (cost leadership strategy)

Table 19 shows the final decision statement that includes the option(s) with the highest total weighted scores when added. This option will be recommended for implementation; thus, it is important to state the final decision rather than simply highlighting the winning option(s).

Table 18.   Decision Matrix 4.

Current Reality: Skye Construction is experiencing a decline in revenue as evidenced by a decrease in productivity and unstable sales growth
Decision Analysis Statement: Determine the best approach to reverse declining revenues

Strategy-based Objectives	WT	A SC	A WT SC	B SC	B WT SC	C SC	C WT SC	D SC	D WT SC
1. Maximize profit	10	10	100	7	70	7	70	9	90
2. Improve workplace environment	10	3	30	2	20	8	80	5	50
3. Maximize relationships strategic partners	9	10	90	10	90	7	63	10	90
4. Differentiate products and services from competitors	9	7	63	5	45	10	90	4	36
5. Maximize the utilization of the current capabilities	8	4	32	10	80	0	0	10	80
6. Maximize social media presence	7	7	49	8	56	9	63	0	0
Total weighted scores			373		361		366		346

Final decision:

Strategic Options Legend:
A = Reduce amount of time to complete projects (differentiation strategy)
B = Partner with complementors
C = Improve branding
D = Find cheaper materials (cost leadership strategy)

A strategic option is viable only if the company can make it happen. Once the decision has been made, the problem solvers should be prepared to discuss how the option would affect each functional area, specifically the area that will play the biggest role in its successful implementation.

Table 19.   Decision Matrix 5.

Current Reality: Skye Construction is experiencing a decline in revenue as evidenced by a decrease in productivity and unstable sales growth
Decision Analysis Statement: Determine the best approach to reverse declining revenues

Strategy-Based Objectives	WT	A SC	A WT SC	B SC	B WT SC	C SC	C WT SC	D SC	D WT SC
1. Maximize profit	10	10	100	7	70	7	70	9	90
2. Improve workplace environment	10	3	30	2	20	8	80	5	50
3. Maximize relationships strategic partners	9	10	90	10	90	7	63	10	90
4. Differentiate products and services from competitors	9	8	72	5	45	10	90	4	36
5. Maximize the utilization of the current capabilities	8	4	32	10	80	0	0	10	80
6. Maximize social media presence	7	7	49	8	56	9	63	0	0
Total weighted scores			373		361		366		346

Final decision: Reverse declining revenues by reducing amount of time to complete projects and improved branding

Strategic Options Legend:
A = Reduce amount of time to complete projects (differentiation strategy)
B = Partner with complementors
C = Improve branding
D = Find cheaper materials (cost leadership strategy)

Play scripting or acting out the scenarios can be very effective in depicting potential outcomes and providing examples of how things can go well or go awry. It is useful irrespective of whether significant changes are expected. It serves more as a training tool for problem solvers at any level, but it requires knowledge and insight into a business environment. When participants are not comfortable role-playing, paid or professional actors can be brought in to demonstrate the key points. Likewise, if the company chooses, professional playwrights working alongside problem solvers can develop a convincing script that will surely keep the stakeholders' attention. Additionally, potential problems and their likely causes will be addressed as part of implementation planning.

SECTION C

ORGANIZATIONAL LEARNING THROUGH STRATEGY IMPLEMENTATION

Business students are often exposed to the strategic management process through analyzing cases. However, strategic management is not like analyzing a case study where much of the work has been done for you and you simply propose the presumed most effective solution using supporting evidence. What appears to be a realistic solution could be great on paper but falls apart as the team puts it into action. To really understand a business process and become proficient in performing the activities undertaken to accomplish an outcome, you have to learn by doing. As each problem solver and contributor learns, his or her new knowledge informs the organization, and thus the organization learns.

A crucial part of Phase 5 is to ensure that organizational learning is an expectation during Phase 6 of the strategic management process, or strategy implementation involves putting the proposed strategy into action, tracking its progress, and adjusting to ensure its success. One cannot imagine all of the things that could need adjusting in the planning process; thus, planning, and real-time decision making is the key to keeping a strategic plan on track. Documenting those adjustments and sharing them with others lead to organizational learning that can be applied to future strategy making efforts.

8

LINKING IMPLEMENTATION
TO PLAN OBJECTIVES

Implementation planning is part of Phase 5 (Fig. 4). Implementation planning is the process by which a detailed recommendation for how to put a strategy into action is developed. It involves identifying the activities that are recommended for successful outcomes. Two terms are often used to refer to these activities: tactics and components. When referring to a strategy, strategists use the term tactic that is one activity in the strategy. When referring to an implementation plan, one activity in the plan is commonly referred to as a component. Again, these terms are interchangeable. For example, Activity Planned could be written as Component Planned or Tactic Planned. Consistency is essential to ensuring that your audience understands your message. Within the implementation plan are subplans and worksheets that help to eliminate activities that do not support the desired outcomes. Subplans are "mini" implementation plans that provide the problem solvers and contributors with additional activities that should be done to ensure the success of a particular component.

Implementation planning consists of 10 steps:

Step 1 is developing an Implementation Plan Statement that drives the plan. This step begins by thoughtfully considering and summarizing feedback from the Decision Analysis and the presentation to key leaders and ensuring the final decision statement reflects the strategic option(s) that was approved (not merely recommended) for implementation by the key decision makers. The Implementation Plan Statement must be tied to their final decision and not the final decision in the Decision Matrix as the decision maker's decision supersedes the work that went into the Decision Analysis.

Step 2 is identifying three objectives for the Implementation Plan. The three plan objectives should include an intentional consideration of the company's constraints on talent, time, and money. These are not strategy-based objectives but objectives that will determine if the Implementation Plan is effective. All strategy-based objectives should have been considered in the Decision Analysis and appear in the decision matrix or Appendix.

Step 3 is identifying the components/tactics/activities that must be completed to meet the objectives and put the strategy into action. Given the number could be lengthy; it is best practice to present the primary components/tactics/activities as part of an overall plan and include subcomponents/tasks/sub-activities in a subplan when needed. The components of the plan and subsequent subplans should be listed chronologically when the order of completion matters.

Step 4 is considering and addressing potential problems that may arise. Most if not all potential problems were to be considered during the decision making phase. However, in this step, a detailed plan is developed to address each potential problem. A failure to do this step indicates that the problem solvers deem the plan to be foolproof and guaranteed to succeed.

Step 5 is confirming that the company has the human resources (knowledge, skills, and abilities) and materials necessary to put the plan into action and develop subplans as needed. In cases where the firm cannot identify internal resources, outsourcing is necessary and the contact information and other pertinent information that explains the need to use external sources should be provided.

Step 6 is setting timelines for the completion of the entire plan and each activity.

Step 7 is providing cost estimates for all components, tactics, and activities required that have a cost (no matter how large or small) with the allotted budget in mind.

Step 8 is reviewing the plan to determine its potential to be effective in meeting the objectives set out in Step 2.

Step 9 is presenting the draft of the plan to the decision makers for input and commitment. Adjust as necessary. Clearly communicate the process and procedures that went into the development of the draft and future steps to finalize the plan.

Step 10 is providing ongoing modification of the plan as needed throughout the implementation process.

Only in organizations of one are all steps intended to be handled by one individual as a best practice. More on the import of this assumption is explained in Part II, Chapter 9.

Next, let us explore how we can implement the strategy identified in the decision analysis in Skye Construction.

FINDINGS FROM SKYE CONSTRUCTION

The task force was excited to learn that the key decision makers were pleased with their recommendation to reverse declining revenues by using a differentiation strategy based on reducing the amount of time to complete projects and improved branding. As shown in Tables 20–27, they worked collaboratively to develop a plan to put the recommendation into action. The CEO gave them three weeks to come up with an implementation plan. They were told the plan had two requirements: implementation had to be completed within three months (no later than June 30), and they had a budget of $300,000. The member from Human Resources asked if there were any guidelines in terms of hiring new staff. The CEO committed to hiring two people whose salary would not be part of the budget. As shown in Table 20, three plan objectives were identified. The overall plan statement and objectives are included in the subsequent tables and are repeated in all subplans.

Plan Statement and Objectives

Next, the task force brainstormed about the activities needed to make this strategy work. In Table 21, notice how they isolated the major activities needed and put them in chronological order. They included a column to show whether an activity was aligned to either strategic option A or C or both from the decision analysis. Of course, this column would not have been necessary if they had selected only one option.

Table 20.   Implementation Plan Objectives.

Plan Statement: Develop the best implementation plan to reverse declining revenues by reducing the amount of time to complete projects and improved branding

Objectives:

1. The majority of the work must be completed by current staff. Only two new hires allowed

2. Plan must be fully operational/completed by June 30, YEAR

3. Cannot spend more than $300,000

They also identified who is responsible for carrying out each. Here, they could have included the name, title, and contact information for an expert in the firm or the name, title, company, and contact information for an external expert. In cases where more details were necessary, they developed subplans and worksheets to guide the implementation process. The contact information for the person responsible for an activity is only required once in the tables. However, it is a good practice to include a contact list of all persons/department or unit leaders responsible for activities in the plan in the Appendix.

The first two components represent a commitment to organizational learning, questioning the status quo.

IMPLEMENTATION PLAN COMPONENTS AND RESPONSIBILITY LIST

Subplans

Based on their brainstorming session, as shown in Table 22, the task force chose to develop a subplan for two components: E and F (*note: neither of these requires a subplan. However, for illustrative purposes, I show how a subplan can be helpful*). Components E and F involve training problem solvers to ensure they are competent to do the work that is needed later in the implementation plan. Given both components address training needs and only nine activities are involved, rather than develop two separate tables, the task force combined the subplans.

Table 21. Implementation Plan Components and Responsibility List.

Plan Statement: Develop the best implementation plan to reverse declining revenues by reducing the amount of time to complete projects and improved branding
Objective 1: Talent – Only two new hires allowed (abbreviated)
Objective 2: Time – Plan must be fully operational by June 30, YEAR
Objective 3: Budget – $300,000 available to spend

Component/Tactic/Activity		Who	Strategic Options
A	Determine additional capacity of existing accounts	Finance	A
B	Elimination of non-value-added tasks that cause delays	Operations	A
C	Make necessary upgrades to machinery and equipment	Operations	A, C
D	Based on needs found in A, B, C hire up to two additional problem solvers	Human resources Operations Sales	A, C
E	Enhance the knowledge of everyone throughout the company on LEED	R&D	A, C
F	Hold refresher training for marketing and salespeople	Victoria Desta Training specialist LEED (XXX) XXX-XXXX	A, C
G	Develop a standard partnership agreement	Legal	A
H	Attract stakeholders with selective interest in incentives to getting project done efficiently	Sales	A, C
I	Notify current customers about changes and incentives	Strategic communications	C

Strategic Options Legend:
A = Reduce amount of time to complete projects (differentiation strategy)
C = Improve branding

Accepted Risk can be noted with the presence of ✓ (checkmarks), X/Y (Yes) or N(No) as long as it is consistently identified and explained. When an activity has low or acceptable risk, no contingency plan is necessary. However, in cases where there is unacceptable risk, a contingency plan, including preventive measures, is needed.

Table 22.   Implementation Plan Subcomponents and Responsibility List.

Plan Statement:
Develop the best implementation plan to reverse declining revenues by reducing the
time required to complete projects and improved branding
Objective 1: Talent – Only 2 new hires allowed
Objective 2: Time – Plan must be fully operational by June 30, YEAR
Objective 3: Budget – $300,000 available to spend

Subplan Statement: Develop the best training plans for this project

Components		Who?
E	Enhance the knowledge of everyone throughout the company on LEED	R&D
E1	Hold a conference call with managers in-volved about the scope of the training and identify any concerns that will need to be addressed in the training	Director of R&D
E2	Develop a webinar and associated materials	Strategic communications
E3	Send out associated materials via email	Strategic communications
E4	Hold the webinar and take questions	Director of R&D
E5	Develop and send out new materials as appropriate based on the webinar	Strategic communications
F	Hold refresher training for marketing and salespeople	Victoria Desta (outsourced)
F1	Work with firm to develop the strategic message to be conveyed	Director of sales
F2	Set times and dates for training at each state office	Director of Sales
F3	Make travel and meeting arrangements	Sales Office Administrator
F4	Ensure training materials (PowerPoint presentations, videos, DVDs, handouts, etc.) are tailored for Skye Construction	Victoria Desta

Legend for Implementation Planning:
P = Probability of occurrence
S = Seriousness if problem occurs
L = Low
M = Moderate
H = High
Who = Person/Unit/Firm best suited to handle a responsibility and will be held account-able for results
AR = Accepted risk when the risk involved does not warrant attention to avoid it
RP = Residual probability is the likelihood that the preventative action will not work. The
response to this should always be L (Low)
PT = Proactive trigger
RT = Reactive trigger

RISK MANAGEMENT AND STICKING TO THE PLAN

Part of crafting strategy is taking risks and considering that something could not go as planned. A risk is a possibility that an unwanted outcome will happen as the result of poor decision making or that something will happen that can negatively impact expected outcomes. Every day, we take risks based on assumptions of how things will turn out when we act.

For example, something as simple as crossing the street when the street signal indicates that it is safe to do so requires that you assume that the cars approaching that street will adhere to the signal and stop so that you can safely cross the street. On most days, you make it across to the other side. On the days when you almost don't make it, you think about the choices you made simply by crossing the street and hope the driver was insured against risk. Certainly, there is a possibility that a distracted driver does not see the signal, or a driver refuses to adhere to the signal, or a driver is unable to stop before the automobile crashes into you. As in this everyday example, in business, on most days things turn out as planned. However, on those days when things do not, you have to consider the consequences of what could go wrong and the implications of acting on your decisions.

Risk-averse decision makers tend to play it safe. However, risk takers embrace opportunities that are not safe. Most problem solvers take calculated risks based on the expected outcomes. A risked outcome is the same as a potential problem. Here are some ways to respond to risk:

- *accept the risk* – if the organization can tolerate the impact of the risked outcome/potential problem or if the cost to remove the risk is prohibitive;

- *monitor the risk* – if the risked outcome/potential problem is unlikely to occur;

- *avoid the risk* – do not include the activity that leads to the risked outcome/potential problem if the activity can be isolated;

- *outsource the risk* – assign the responsibility for the risked outcome/potential problem to a third party; and

- *mitigate the risk* – eliminate or minimize the risk involved in the activity that leads to the risked outcome/potential problem.

Minimizing risk during implementation planning allows contributors to stick to the plan during actual implementation.

AVOIDING POTENTIAL PROBLEMS

At best, strategic thinking helps prepare the organization for future challenges given the difficulty of predicting *exactly* how things will evolve in business. Understanding or anticipating what will happen in the future is not easy. Gaining alignment between key decision makers about how to prepare for the future can be as difficult.

Step 4 in implementation planning is attempting to avoid potential problems before they arise. A Potential Problem Avoidance Analysis can be used to analyze activities where there is a risk of failure and to determine (1) if that activity should be avoided or (2) if there are additional activities that can be included that will reduce the likelihood that the problem would occur and its severity if it does occur.

Staffing requirements or competency of the person(s) assigned to perform an activity should not be considered as a potential problem. The assumption is that the people who have been assigned will get it done (effectively) and get it done on time (efficiently). When it is evident that something will not get done or something will not get done on time; replacing the person assigned to the activity may be the best way to address the problem. As such, for internal assignments, additional training may be necessary prior to bringing them on board the project. For outsourced activities, legal agreements should eliminate competency issues.

The Potential Problem Avoidance Analysis has five steps:

Step 1 is providing a Potential Problem Avoidance Statement that expresses what the problem solver seeks to accomplish. It should be directly tied to the statement used in the Implementation Plan.

Step 2 is identifying potential problems that can occur when implementing each plan component and assessing the risk if the potential problem(s) were to occur. Base the analysis on the probability that a problem will occur and if it does, what is the level of seriousness (severity)? Only those potential problems that the firm is unwilling to accept the risk (tolerate) are worthy of further consideration in the analysis. This can be accomplished through using both a cost and value perspective where the problem solver assesses whether it is worth the time and money to address the issue. Notations include: P = Probability. S = Seriousness. AR = Accepted Risk. Probability and Seriousness are notated as L (Low – It is no big deal), M (Moderate – some concern but manageable), and H (High – This would be catastrophic to the project). Accepted Risk can be noted with the presence of checkmarks, (✓), X or Y (Yes) as long as it is consistently applied and explained). Using Y (Yes) *and* N (No) in the same table is not recommended, as it requires more work for the person developing the plan and not doing so makes it easier for the person considering the plan to read and understand the choice.

Step 3 is identifying the likely causes of the potential problems identified in Step 2 and assessing the risk if each likely cause were to occur. Only those likely causes of potential problems that the firm is unwilling to accept the risk (tolerate) are worthy of further consideration in the analysis. The same notations in Step 2 apply.

Step 4 is developing actions to prevent the likely causes that were intolerable in Step 3 and identifying two protective triggers (one proactive and the other reactive) that would indicate that something is not going as planned and/or the preventive actions may not or have not worked.

Step 5 is developing contingent actions to be put in place when it is determined that the preventive action has been or may be ineffective.

Note that Step 3 is where organizational learning is most noticeable. Individuals throughout the organization must reflect on company policies and practices that could hinder the success of the plan. It is an opportunity for managers and contributors in functional areas to rethink how they get work done and to reengineer their work processes. Additional concerns will likely surface during the actual implementation phase, but taking a proactive approach sends a message to everyone that efforts should be made to change or improve those processes that do not support the new strategy. Moreover, it is an opportunity to encourage risk taking and learning from mistakes and failures as learning opportunities for discovery.

When a risk has been minimized, the remaining risk is referred to as the residual probability that the risked outcome will occur or the probability that the preventive measure put in place will not work. The decision makers should agree on contingencies and what events will trigger the need for them to be put into place. Contingencies are actions that are put in place when a risked outcome is probable. A contingency should align with the chosen strategy. It is not meant to abandon a strategy but to ensure that the strategy is not derailed during implementation.

Next, let us explore how we can identify and address some of the potential problems that can arise as we implement our strategy in Skye Construction.

FINDINGS FROM SKYE CONSTRUCTION

As a result of the brainstorming session, the task force is somewhat confident that the plan they will present to the decision makers will work and thus be approved. However, they realize that some activities may not go as planned. Thus, they determined that a Potential Problem Avoidance Analysis is needed. Table 23 reveals a list of the potential problems that were identified. At the top of the table is the Potential Problem Avoidance Statement. Next, each of the identified potential problems is listed on the left, with an associated letter as a marker. To show that some potential problems were associated, they marked them with the same letter with a number that isolates them as separate potential problems. The next two columns reflect how the team assessed the probability and seriousness of each potential problem as either: L (low), M (moderate), or H (high). As an alternative, headers for the probability and seriousness columns could have been shown as "P" or "S," respectively. To the far right in the last column, is accepted risk. In this column, the team placed a check (✓) in a cell to show that they deemed the risk of that specific potential problem (based on the probability and seriousness) was insignificant. Absence of a check signals that the team was not willing to accept the risk or willing to risk the impact of that potential problem.

Of the five potential problems the task force identified, two potential problems were significant enough that the task force wasn't willing to accept the risk: A and B1. As shown in Table 23 given there is check (✓), both of

Table 23. Potential Problem Avoidance Analysis Accepted Risk.

Potential Problem Avoidance Analysis

Potential Problem Avoidance Statement: Develop the best contingency plan to avoid potential problems with the plan to reverse declining revenues by reducing the amount of time to complete projects and improve branding

	Potential Problems	Probability	Seriousness	Accepted Risk
A	Stakeholders are unwilling to spend more for LEED products	M	H	
B1	Upgrades to machinery and equipment may be too costly at this time	M	H	
B2	Outsourcing training is not within budget	L	M	✓
C	Competitive energy programs become more attractive for to partners	L	M	✓
D	Sales team can't attend training	L	L	✓

these potential problems were assessed as serious if they were to happen and the probability of them happening was considered to be moderate.

Once the task force determined which potential problems were significant and warranted further attention, in similarly developed tables, they identified the likely causes of those specific potential problems. The likely causes for each potential problem identified are listed in a separate table.

Tables 24 and 25 reflect their analysis for potential problems A and B1. Again, a check (✓) in a cell under Accepted Risk indicates that the likely cause was not deemed significant enough to warrant further attention in the analysis.

Once the team identified and assessed the likely causes, they built contingency tables to show what actions would be taken to ensure those likely causes would not derail the plan's success. The number of contingency tables required is based on the number of likely causes that were deemed significant (where risk was a factor). Each likely cause for each potential problem that was considered needs its own contingency table.

In Tables 26 and 27, the task force reminds us of the potential problem that was of concern and how it was assessed for probability and seriousness.

Table 24. Potential Problem Avoidance Analysis: Likely Causes of Potential Problem A.

Potential Problem Avoidance Statement: Develop the best contingency plan to avoid potential problems with the plan to reverse declining revenues by reducing the amount of time to complete projects and improve branding

A	Potential Problem: Stakeholders are unwilling to spend more for LEED products	P M	S H	Probability	Seriousness	Accepted Risk
Likely Causes						
1	We target the wrong partners and buyers			L	H	✓
2	Stakeholders are skeptical about products. They do not see value					
3	Inflexible sales pitch			L	M	✓
4	New equipment drives up costs			M	H	
5	Buyers can't get funding			L	H	✓

It lists the likely cause that is being addressed and its probability. They also include columns for preventive actions, who is responsible for carrying out an activity (in this case initials, rather than full names), and the residual probability that the preventive action is expected to work. Lastly, there is a row of cells for the contingent action, the triggers that will determine if the contingent action will be put in place, and who is responsible for addressing the triggers.

Table 25.   Potential Problem Avoidance Analysis: Likely Causes of Potential Problem B1.

Potential Problem Avoidance Statement: Develop the best contingency plan to avoid potential problems with the plan to reverse declining revenues by reducing the amount of time to complete projects and improve branding

B1	*Potential Problem*: Upgrades to machinery and equipment may be too costly at this time	P M	S H	Probability	Seriousness	Accepted Risk
Likely Causes						
1	Can't get discounted new equipment			M	H	
2	Loan structure is too prohibitive			M	M	
3	Cost/benefit of new features does not justify added expense			M	L	✓
4	Management is unwilling to increase budget			L	M	✓

**Table 26.   Potential Problem Avoidance Analysis: Contingency Planning
for Potential Problem A.**

Potential Problem Avoidance Statement: Develop the best contingency plan to avoid
potential problems with the plan to reverse declining revenues by reducing the amount
of time to complete projects and improve branding

A	*Potential Problem*: Stakeholders are unwilling to spend more for LEED products			P M	S H
Likely Causes		P	Preventive Actions	Who	RP
2	Stakeholders are skeptical about products. They do not see value.	M	Develop new stakeholder-specific marketing materials with information on LEED	LH	L
4	New equipment drives up costs	M	Trade in old equipment	SCM	L

Contingent Action A:
Redirect search and focus on
acquiring new clients who can
afford price demanded.

Triggers A: BSE
PT: Closely monitor
outcomes of sales team
for first 30 days
RT: Failure to achieve 20%
increase in revenue within
in 60 days of launch

Table 27. Potential Problem Avoidance Analysis: Contingency Planning for Potential Problem B1.

Potential Problem Avoidance Statement: Develop the best contingency plan to avoid potential problems with the plan to reverse declining revenues by reducing the amount of time to complete projects and improve branding

B1	Upgrades to machinery and equipment may be too costly at this time			P M	S H
Likely Causes		P	Preventive Action	Who	RP
1	Can't get discounted new equipment	M	Get multiple quotes, including quotes on equipment that is newer but used	SCM	L
2	Loan structure Loan structure is too prohibitive	M	Use cash to lower interest payments	SP	L

Contingent Action B1:	Triggers B1:	SCM
Get best financing terms now and refinance as balance decreases	RT: Quotes are too high	SP
	PT: Call creditor and ask for assistance	

As a result of the Potential Problem Avoidance Analysis, the team is confident that if the problem solvers follow the plan they have developed, Skye Construction will be able to reverse its declining revenues. However, they know that their planning is not yet complete. They must ensure that the plan meets the objectives set by the CEO.

9

MANAGING TALENT, TIME, AND MONEY

A well-thought-out implementation plan allows companies to put their resources to best use and to find ways to offset constraints to meet strategy-based objectives. Once the components have been identified and potential problems have been considered, recall that the next step in implementation planning is to address the objectives (outlined in Step 2) for talent, time, and money covered in Steps 5, 6, and 7:

Step 5 is confirming that the company has the human resources (knowledge, skills, and abilities) and materials necessary to put the plan into action and develop subplans as needed.

Step 6 is setting timelines for completion of the entire plan and each activity.

Step 7 is providing cost estimates for all components/tactics/activities required that have a cost (no matter how large or small) with the allotted budget in mind.

Once problem solvers complete steps 5, 6, and 7, how will they know the developed Implementation Plan is comprehensive and is of value- thus, likely to be approved? This question is addressed by moving to Step 8 in the implementation planning process:

Step 8 is reviewing the plan to determine its potential to be effective in meeting the objectives set out in Step 2.

In order to complete Step 8, problem solvers can use the following checklist to ensure the Implementation Plan meets its objectives and confirm that each objective is adequately addressed:

✓ *Have we spelled out the roles of everyone in the plan and tied their activities to the desired results?* To test a talent objective, look within the components of the implementation plan to see if tactics to meet that objective have been included. Components of the implementation plan should include talent requirements and when necessary, subplans should be developed.

✓ *Does the plan meet the deadline set by key decision makers?* To ensure the plan meets its time objective, create an event schedule to make certain every component can be completed within the time constraints. To test a time objective, look at the event schedule to determine if every component is scheduled to be completed prior to the deadline.

✓ *Is the plan within budget?* To ensure that a plan meets the budget objective, identify activities that have a financial obligation and be prepared to negotiate prices to stay within the budget. To test the budget objective, create a budget test based on the components and subcomponents that had a financial obligation to determine if the plan comes in around budget.

Lastly and most importantly, testing the plan objectives is *not* the same as evaluating plan effectiveness. Testing plan objectives is done prior to implementing the plan to determine if the plan that has been developed has the potential to meet the decision maker(s) expectations. Evaluating plan effectiveness is done during implementation and after the plan has been concluded. A problem solver should be able to answer the question "Does this plan meet its objectives?" when proposing the plan to the decision makers.

ASSESSING TALENT NEEDS

Human resource professionals play a key role in the strategy making process. There are two places within the implementation plan where talent matters - the staffing requirements and determining who will handle the work that has to be done. Determining staffing requirements includes considering the level of staffing required; timing of when the staff will be needed, and addressing what to do when gaps exist between what is needed and what is actual. Determining "who" ensures the problem solver(s) identified to handle a particular task has the specific competencies needed and is empowered to do what is needed to be successful.

There is often a gap between how people perceive themselves (and what they can do) and what they actually achieve. Some people have huge egos and perceive themselves to be indispensable because of past accomplishments. In some cases, they are. However, the human resources staff has a responsibility to provide or arrange adequate training to ensure that no one person is indispensable as that puts the company in jeopardy. The least capable people may think they can do more than they can. Again, it is important to identify strengths and weaknesses of each contributor so his or her competencies match or exceed the job requirements for opportunities. Failure to do so harms the strategy making process. Additionally, as someone who is perceived as a thinking strategist, you must determine when you are poised to make a contribution. Fig. 30 depicts a thought process to help you decide if you should join a team.

STRATEGY IMPLICATIONS OF DIVERSITY, EQUITY, AND INCLUSION

Diverse individuals contribute to the organization's understanding of different products and services needed in target markets. Diversity refers to surface level similarities and differences as well as deep level similarities and differences that ground our personal experiences, values, and worldviews. Surface level diversity includes race, ethnicity, gender, age, religion, language, abilities/disabilities, sexual orientation, socioeconomic status, geographic region, and more. Deep level diversity includes how you differ from others to whom you have similar diversity. It recognizes that people who are similar (e.g., same race, gender, and from the same geographic region) do not all think and behave alike.

In the United States, society has historically shown a preference for White-Christian-heterosexual males, which has led to equity gaps for traditionally

Fig. 30. Managing Individual Contributions.

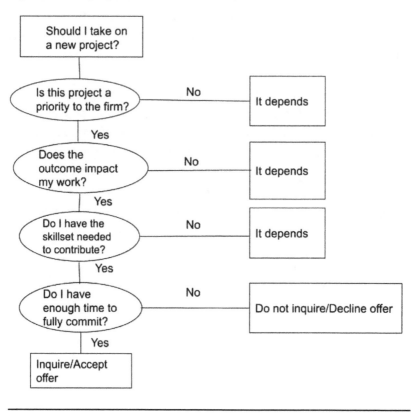

excluded groups. However, forward-thinking companies have implemented diversity, equity, and inclusion (DEI) strategies to close the gap and foster a sense of belonging, dignity, and justice for their stakeholders irrespective of differences. DEI strategies ensure that persons from traditionally excluded groups have what they need to succeed in an organization. Moreover, they are intended to allow everyone to excel and be evaluated on their individual purpose rather than feeling that their actions and thoughts should be similar to those of the dominant group within an organization.

While these organizational efforts may appear altruistic, there is a business case for using a DEI strategy. As noted by Wells, Malik, and Edmondson (2021), not only do these individuals contribute to our understanding of customer needs, but having a good DEI strategy and outcomes allow organizations to use diversity in their branding. Members of traditionally excluded groups should be visible in leadership roles and included in decision making efforts accordingly. For best results, companies should hire ample employees with various differences given not all people in a traditionally excluded group think alike or have had the same personal experience impacting their worldview. Moreover, their difference alone should not imply competence or incompetence.

Every employee should be able to present their authentic self in the workplace and express a personal identity. However, there is a belief that as a diversity hire or appointment, a person's performance impacts all other persons within their diverse group in an organization (and possibly within an ecosystem). While every person is responsible for his or her success, there is a level of trust or expectation that as a collective group, traditionally excluded group members hold one another accountable. There may be pressure among a group to avoid letting individual actions and decisions (i.e., contributions) reflect negatively on others within the group. As a member of an organization that purports to embrace diversity, when you realize that even with your best efforts and continued investment in yourself, you are not attaining your personal goals; it may be necessary to craft or implement an exit plan so that your contributions may be utilized in a more suitable workplace.

DOCUMENTING CONTRIBUTIONS

Lastly, to ensure that contributors get credit for their work, a Team Contribution Worksheet and Individual Contribution Worksheet are recommended as shown in Tables 28 and 29. The Team Contribution Worksheet shows the work of everyone on the team. Tactics or the activities that are included in the implementation plan are isolated and then the team agrees on who the task should be assigned to and the date task each should be completed. Once the plan is underway, additional details may be added given some details may be missing or unknown at the time the plan is developed. Any deviations from what was planned should be captured including when someone is not able to meet a deadline or is unable to get the work done effectively. Including the information sources demonstrates that the team conducted research when needed rather than relying on their own knowledge or experience.

Table 28. Team Contribution Worksheet.

Plan Statement:
Objective 1: Talent
Objective 2: Time
Objective 3: Budget

Tactic	Who	Planned Date	Actual Date	Cause of Deviation	Information Source

While optional, an Individual Contribution Worksheet allows team members to keep track of tactics that were assigned to them personally and those they volunteered to handle. A check (✓) in a cell under Volunteered indicates that the tactic was something the contributor was not assigned to handle. This column may not be included on the Team Contribution Worksheet because on a team it is expected that individuals will volunteer to assist and tracking that effort is not necessary or collegial. However, for individual accountability, tracking efforts to assist the team by the contributor helps to clarify individual effort just in case claims of free riding arise and this detail

Table 29. Individual Contribution Worksheet.

Your Name

Your Role (Area of Expertise)

Plan Statement:
Objective 1: Talent
Objective 2: Time
Objective 3: Budget

Tactic	Volunteered Y or N	Planned Date	Actual Date	Cause of Deviation	Information Source	Additional Notes

can also be used as supporting evidence in a self-assessment for an employee evaluation. Furthermore, the addition of the note's column enables the contributor to include a narrative about the work which might include feedback from team members, decision makers, or personal observations about the handling of a specific tactic.

SETTING REALISTIC TIME EXPECTATIONS

Setting timelines for completion or scheduling times for activities to occur (Step 6 in Implementation Planning) helps to outline particular time windows for when activities are planned to be completed. In the overall plan, time periods for activities or components are scheduled according to the first or second two weeks (half) of the month. In a subplan, the time period for activities or components is set by weeks. In months when five weeks rather than four exist, the time period may show a fifth week, or the time period can be determined by the week that holds the majority of days. For example, if the fifth week ends on Monday, then it may be best to only show four weeks in the schedule. However, if the fifth week ends on Thursday; then it is best to show five weeks. The fifth week is usually included in the second time period when the subplans are part of the overall plan. Lastly, when plans expand beyond one year, the years should be included in the Time Period.

These time schedules depict the anticipated progression of the plan from the beginning until the end. Here's an area where managers often overpromise and underdeliver. While these tools help to set expectations, if they are not set based on what is happening in the organization and industry, the likelihood of failure to meet the plan objectives increases. Managers often set aggressive schedules in hopes that problem solvers can get things done efficiently and effectively, with a major emphasis on efficiency. Normal patterns of activity should not be ignored. For example: during May of each year, the people who are assigned to this plan attend a huge industry convention. As a result, the plan should reflect that work that can be done at the convention only if the convention is a good place to do this work (i.e., networking opportunities, product displays). However, work that is a distraction from the convention should be halted until the contributors return.

Additionally, if there are not enough contributors working on the plan or if one person is responsible for a large portion of the plan, this factor may put the strategy in jeopardy as it may be too much for one person to realistically handle in the time period. If someone is assigned too little responsibility, that observation may signal incompetency or a need to assign more duties if that person is able to handle more work. Balancing the workload, while holding people accountable, helps to make sure the plan and each activity are completed on time.

Thus, in addition to the Plan Schedule, a Time Allocation Schedule (TAS) shows when people or departments have time commitments in the plan. The TAS helps to ease the mind of contributors who sense the proposed plan may demand too much of their time at inopportune times. Alternatively, a Gantt chart, a bar chart that focuses on the activities and the time required to complete them rather than who is responsible for doing the work, may be preferred by decision makers. The advantage to using a Gantt chart is they are helpful in updating progress once the plan is underway. Conversely, TASs are used mainly during the implementation planning phase.

STAYING WITHIN BUDGET

Often budgets drive strategy (Abernethy & Brownell, 1999). When budgets are set, problem solvers strive to identify strategies and tactics that will not exceed the amount that has been set aside. Traditionally, when revenues are up, new programs and products are introduced and funded. When revenues are down, there is typically a reduction to current programs and no new products are introduced. Managers might have to defend their budget requests and not all requests survive. Products or services that are no longer cost-effective may be eliminated.

Budgets are givens (a factor not controlled by the implementers) and constraints (limit what can be done). They drive many of the approaches that companies use to compete. Surely, in most companies, the amount of money available to spend is a factor in decision making. Deliberations on where the money should be spent and how much should be allocated to an activity may lead to several budget iterations until there is consensus at the table.

Plans with low budgets often rely heavily on the intellectual capital (knowledge and applied experience) of the contributors doing the work. Managing intellectual capital well is a sign of good decision making. Having the ability to get things done cheaper or at no cost saves companies money and enables them to compete for opportunities that often require money beyond their means. The conundrum here is if your intellectual capital saves money, what happens to the money that has been allocated but is no longer needed?

Once the budget has been decided, staying within it has two ramifications:

1) *Going over budget may signal poor decision making.* If you spend more money than what has been allocated, the money has to come from another activity in the plan or the plan's budget has to be increased. Rather than going over budget, you can request additional money prior to spending it and hope for a positive response. Or you can spend the money and hope that it is in the overall plan budget and that no activity is disadvantaged or eliminated because of your decision.

2) *Not using your entire budget may signal poor decision making.* Some managers fear if they don't use their entire allotment, they will receive a lower amount in the next budget cycle. In best case scenarios, that would only happen when intellectual capital gained from this experience can be measured and replicated going forward. Thus, the additional funds are no longer needed.

TESTING PLAN OBJECTIVES

Prior to implementing a plan, the contributors should assess its value. Does it best position those who will be involved in putting it into action based on the plan objectives? When any of the plan objectives are not met, a rationale should be included. Remember, this test does not determine if the performance objectives are met. It only tests the Implementation Plan to ensure that it includes the components that could satisfy the Plan objectives. Performance objectives are evaluated after the plan has been fully implemented. Next, let us test our work to see if it met the three objectives identified for Skye Construction's plan:

1. The majority of the work must be completed by current staff. Only two new hires are allowed.

2. Plan must be fully operational by June 30, YEAR

3. Cannot spend more than $300,000.

FINDINGS FROM SKYE CONSTRUCTION

Prior to presenting the Implementation Plan to the decision makers, the task force must review it to determine if the plan objectives that were set before the plan was developed have been met. Tables 30–34 and Fig. 31 show how to test for the three plan objectives:

TESTING THE TALENT OBJECTIVE

Testing the first objective requires an examination of the plan to determine if:

1) every activity has a person assigned to it;

2) the person assigned is currently on board unless an activity is out-sourced; and

3) new hires are needed.

Recall the components listed in the Implementation Plan Components List. As shown in Table 30, if new hires are needed, the need should be clearly pointed out and in this case, confirmation that there are no more than two occurrences as the CEO agreed to hire two new people, but the cost of those hires are not included in the budget. On the other hand, the task force may be able to point out that although they recommended more than two new hires, the projected costs of the new hires will be balanced out by the number of people who are no longer needed because their jobs or contributions have been eliminated as part of a component. In these cases, it must be clear whether the affected contributors will be transferred or terminated.

A transfer does not eliminate the wage cost to the company. While it has a positive impact on the strategic option that is under consideration, a transfer impacts the budget of the transfer unit. Thus, the task force determined further consideration is needed regardless of if the money comes out of this budget.

Table 30.   Implementation Plan Objective Test for Talent.

Plan Statement: Develop the best implementation plan to reverse declining revenues by reducing time required to complete projects and improved branding

Objective 1: Talent – The majority of the work must be completed by current staff. Only two new hires allowed

Component/Tactic/Activity		Who	Strategic Options
A	Determine additional capacity of existing accounts	Finance (new hire)	A
B	Elimination of non-value-added tasks that cause delays	Operations (may be able to eliminate position)	A
C	Make necessary upgrades to machinery and equipment	Operations	A, C
D	Based on needs found in A, B, C hire up to two additional problem solvers	Human resources Operations Sales	A, C
E	Enhance the knowledge of everyone throughout the company on LEED	R&D	A, C
F	Train marketing and salespeople to promote benefits of LEED portfolio	Victoria Desta Training specialist LEED (XXX) XXX-XXXX	A, C
G	Develop a standard partnership agreement	Legal	A
H	Attract stakeholders with selective interest in incentives to getting project done efficiently	Sales (new hire)	A, C
I	Notify current customers about changes and incentives	Strategic communications	C

Legend for Strategic Options:
A = Reduce amount of time to complete projects
C = Improve branding

TESTING THE TIME OBJECTIVE

To determine if the plan meets its time constraints, the task force developed a Plan Schedule Worksheet and a Time Allocation Schedule to set and manage completion expectations as shown in Table 31. Looking at their Plan Schedule Worksheet, it is clear that they plan to have this plan underway between January and June of the current year. If the activities are listed in chronological order on the Implementation Plan Component List, the activities will be scheduled in chronological order unless they are recommended to be completed simultaneously. A legend that identifies each component eliminates the need for returning to the list itself.

For clarity:

Components A and B are recommended to start in the first two weeks of January. Component A should be finished in the second two weeks of January. Component B is expected to be completed no later than the second two weeks of February.

Table 31. Implementation Plan Objective Test for Time.

PLAN OBJECTIVE TEST

OBJECTIVE 2

Plan Statement: Develop the best plan to reverse declining revenues by reducing the time required to complete projects, and improve branding.

Objective 2: Time – Plan must be fully operational by June 30, YEAR

TIME PERIOD	ACTIVITY PLANNED		ACTIVITY ACTUAL		Cause of Deviation? Cost Saved or Incurred
	Start	Finish	Start	Finish	
Jan I	A, B				
Jan II		A			
Feb I	C				
Feb II		B			
Mar I	D				
Mar II	E	C			
Apr I		D			
Apr II		E			
May I	F, G				

Table 31. (*Continued*)

May II		G
Jun I	H, I	F
Jun II		H, I

Legends for Implementation Planning:
Time Period Legend:
I = First two weeks of the month
II = Second two weeks of the month

Component Legend:
A = Determine additional capacity of existing accounts
B = Elimination of non-value-added tasks that cause delays
C = Make necessary upgrades to machinery and equipment
D = Based on needs found in A, B, C hire up to two additional problem solvers
E = Enhance the knowledge of everyone throughout the company on LEED
F = Hold refresher training for marketing and salespeople
G = Develop a standard partnership agreement
H = Attract stakeholders with selective interest in incentives to getting project done
    efficiently
I = Notify current customers about changes and incentives

Table 32.   Implementation Plan Objective Test for Time for Subplans.

Plan Statement: Develop the best plan to reverse declining revenues by reducing the
time required to complete projects, and improve branding.

Objective 2: Time – Plan must be fully operational by June 30, YEAR

TIME PERIOD	ACTIVITY PLANNED		ACTIVITY ACTUAL		Cause of Deviation? Cost Saved or Incurred
	Start	Finish	Start	Finish	
March 4	E1				
April 1	E2	E1			
April 2		E2			
April 3	E3	E3,			
April 4	E4, E5	E3, E4			
May 1					
May 2		E5			
May 3	F1	F1			
May 4	F2	F2			
Jun I	F3, F4	F3			
Jun 2		F4			

Table 32. (*Continued*)

Legends for Subplan Implementation Planning
Time Period Legend:
1 = 1st week of the month
2 = 2nd week of the month
3 = 3rd week of the month
4 = 4th week of the month
5 = 5th week of the month

Component Legend:
E = Enhance the knowledge of everyone throughout the company on LEED
F = Hold refresher training for marketing and salespeople

Subcomponent Legend:
E1 = Hold a conference call with managers involved about the scope of the training and identify any concerns that will need to be addressed in the training
E2 = Develop a webinar and associated materials
E3 = Send out associated materials via email
E4 = Hold the webinar and take questions
E5 = Develop and send out new materials as appropriate based on the webinar
F1 = Work with firm to develop the strategic message to be conveyed
F2 = Set times and dates for training at each state office
F3 = Make travel and meeting arrangements
F4 = Ensure training materials (PowerPoint presentations, videos, DVDs, handouts. etc.) are tailored for Skye Construction

Table 33. Implementation Plan Objective Test for Time for Components with Subplans.

Plan Statement: Develop the best plan to reverse declining revenues by reducing the time required to complete projects, and improve branding.

Objective 2: Time – Plan must be fully operational by June 30, YEAR

TIME PERIOD	ACTIVITY PLANNED		ACTIVITY ACTUAL		Cause of Deviation? Cost Saved or Incurred
	Start	Finish	Start	Finish	
Jan I	A,B				
Jan II		A			
Feb I	C				
Feb II		B			
Mar I	D				
Mar II	E	C			
Mar 4	E1				
Apr I		D			
Apr 1	E2	E1			

Table 33. (*Continued*)

Apr 2		E2
Apr II		
Apr 3	E3	
Apr 4	E4, E5	E3, E4
May I		
May 1		
May 2		E5
May II	F	
May 3	F1	F1
May 4	F2	F2
Jun I		
Jun 1	F3. F4, G	F3
Jun 2	H,I	F4, G
Jun II		H, I

Legends for Combined Implementation Planning

Time Period Legend:
I = First two weeks of the month
II = Second two weeks of the month
1 = First week of the month
2 = Second week of the month
3 = Third week of the month
4 = Fourth week of the month
5 = Fifth week of the month

Combined Components Legend:
A = Determine additional capacity of existing accounts
B = Elimination of non-value-added tasks that cause delays
C = Make necessary upgrades to machinery and equipment
D = Based on needs found in A, B, C hire up to two additional problem solvers
E = Enhance the knowledge of everyone throughout the company on LEED
E1 = Hold a conference call with managers involved about the scope of the training and identify any concerns that will need to be addressed in the training
E2 = Develop a webinar and associated materials
E3 = Send out associated materials via email
E4 = Hold the webinar and take questions
E5 = Develop and send out new materials as appropriate based on the webinar
F = Hold refresher training for marketing and salespeople
F1 = Work with firm to develop the strategic message to be conveyed
F2 = Set times and dates for training at each state office
F3 = Make travel and meeting arrangements
F4 = Ensure training materials (PowerPoint presentations, videos, DVDs, handouts. etc.) are tailored for Skye Construction
G = Develop a standard partnership agreement
H = Attract stakeholders with selective interest in incentives to getting project done efficiently
I = Notify current customers about changes and incentives

Subplans

Again, as shown in Table 32, in a subplan, the activities are scheduled by individual weeks rather than by two-week periods. Recall Component E is expected to begin in the first two weeks of March and completed no later than the second two weeks of April. Component F is expected to begin in the first two weeks of May and be completed no later than the first two weeks of June.

For clarity:

Subcomponent E1 is recommended to start in the fourth week of March and be completed no later than the first week of April.

Subcomponent E2 is recommended to start in the first week of April and be completed no later than the second week of April.

Rather than separating out the sub-activities into a Plan Schedule Worksheet of its own, the sub-activities can be included in the overall plan as shown in Table 33.

In this case, the sub-activities are scheduled within the appropriate two-week time periods of its associated activity. Notice that the subcomponents are aligned with the components in the overall plan. Also note, no activities are planned for the first week of May to ensure that the contributors can attend the industry convention.

As the plan is underway, intentional efforts to periodically evaluate the plan to assess its progress and effectiveness are needed and to acknowledge deviations when necessary. Without exception, deviations that incur costs or save money should be noted.

TIME ALLOCATION SCHEDULE

Fig. 31 shows a Time Allocation Schedule used to show the estimated amount of time that each person or unit will be expected to work on the plan. The team was intentional in informing those who played a major role that the maximum recommended time away from their regular duties was four days within a week. Each cell within a week represents one day.

Notice, that although F4 is outsourced, Sales has final responsibility for ensuring the materials are tailored for the company.

Fig. 31. Time Allocation Schedule.

PLAN STATEMENT: Develop the best plan to reverse declining revenues by reducing the time required to complete projects and improved branding. Objective 2: Time - Plan must be fully operational by June 30, YEAR

Table 34. Implementation Plan Objective Test for Budget.

Plan Statement: Develop the best implementation plan to reverse declining revenues by reducing the time required to complete projects and improved branding

Objective 3: Cannot spend more than $300,000

Cost Projections

Components and Subcomponents	Projected Cost	Total Remaining	Actual Cost	Cause of Deviation

Under budget substantially
Over budget
Over budget substantially

TESTING THE BUDGET OBJECTIVE

Table 34 shows how all components in the proposed strategy that will require money from the budget would be shown. Components that are most vital to plan success are listed first. Expected cost should be aligned with the budget.

At the conclusion of its meeting, the task force was able to determine if the plan met the decision makers' objectives and make changes when not.

Objective 1: Talent – The majority of the work must be completed by current staff. Only two new hires allowed as verified through the List of Components

Objective 2: Time – Plan must be fully operational by June 30, YEAR as verified through the Plan Schedule Worksheet.

Objective 3: Budget – should not exceed $300,000 available to spend as verified by Cost Projections.

SECTION D

ASSESSING PROGRESS AND REPORTING IMPACT

Strategic management is a useful process as it gets everyone on the same page and provides opportunities for organizational learning. However, in the end, it is the results that matter. Not only are results evaluated but also the person/team that is responsible for performing the work throughout the process should be evaluated and held accountable.

This section will discuss the art of gaining commitment and evaluating performance. It will also explain different corrective actions that a firm can take when a deviation between planned and actual results exists. Additionally, we will explore how those deviations are communicated.

10

STRATEGY EVALUATION AND CONTROL

Phases 6 and 7 of the strategic management process are interconnected. Phase 6, putting the implementation plan into action and engaging in organizational learning, ensures that necessary changes are made in real time. Step 10 in implementation planning, its final step, is providing ongoing modification of the plan as needed throughout the implementation process. Phase 7, strategy evaluation, the final phase of the strategic management process, is determining whether the plan is meeting/has met performance expectations. When the plan is underway, efforts to ensure that it is going as intended or to determine where, if any, flaws, or miscalculations exist must be undertaken. At the end of these two phases, institutionalizing best practices that were learned in the process improves the company's business model.

IDENTIFYING AND RECORDING DEVIATIONS FROM PLANNED RESULTS

Throughout the implementation phase, information is needed to determine how well the strategy is working. When there is a deviation from what was planned or expected and what actually happened, the decision makers must determine why and what happens next. As Wheelen and Hunger (2012) noted, when there is not sufficient information available to monitor how well things are going, suggest a change to the information system. Additionally, when several people are working on a project, it is a good practice to have a record of things that did not go as planned and why by the person

Fig. 32.   Deviation Tactics.

Preventive Action
Proactive
Before event

Correction
Reactive
At the time

Corrective Action
Prevent reoccurrence
After event

Contingent Action
Prevent derailment
If trigger indicates
additional risk

who was responsible for implementing an activity. A status report would show the deviations from what was planned, feedback if any, the corrections taken, and the corrective actions to ensure that the process allows for better outcomes in the future. While a correction is an immediate response to stop the bleeding, corrective actions are proposed to ensure that the bleeding doesn't happen again. Moreover, preventive actions and contingent actions were discussed in implementation planning. Fig. 32 provides a scenario for how these four deviations and responses relate.

Not all deviations are bad news. For example, if the objective was to increase sales by three percent, but the team was able to increase sales by ten percent, there may be a reason to celebrate. However, this deviation signals there is an issue with the team's ability to anticipate outcomes or set objectives. Certainly, it would be difficult to be exact when setting objectives. Yet, deviations from what was planned and what was accomplished should not be significant. An analysis of what happened and why should lead to real-time adjustments and better decision making in the future.

ACCOUNTABILITY

Not only are results evaluated but the person/team that is responsible for performing the work throughout the process should also be evaluated and held accountable. Accountability is not an evil concept. At its core is ensuring that the activities that need to happen actually happen. Moreover, ensuring that someone is responsible for paying attention to how, when, where, etc. activities are handled, that they are adjusted as needed, and that someone reports back to the rest of the team as needed to ensure that success is not derailed.

Without question, when no one is held accountable, something that was deemed to be covered may fall through the cracks. On the other hand, a reporting out process helps to ensure that attention is paid to detail, progress is being made or issues are being addressed. It is beyond the scope of this book to discuss performance appraisals; however, a performance appraisal should reflect how effectively the activities were handled.

Lastly, when determining how well a company is doing, it is essential to know how much money it is generating, the amount of debt it is incurring, and other factors that can hinder success. Financial statements provide that information. Recall, the conclusions drawn from a competitive financial analysis can be included as either a strength or weakness based on industry rank, annual sales or revenues and ratios of select companies within their strategic group. However, before proceeding to the financial statements, let us consider some common terms that permeate them.

COMMON FINANCIAL TERMS

Below are succinct definitions of some common financial terms. If you will use these terms in a decision making role, if necessary, seek additional training or education. The goal here is that you will have working knowledge of why these terms matter.

Assets: Resources that have value. They may be tangible (physical property, such as plants, trucks, equipment, and inventory, etc.) or intangible (investments, trademarks, patents, intellectual property, etc.).

Cash/Cash Equivalent: Money in hand (Bank Balance – Petty Cash – Receivables – Securities).

Current: Describing a time period within one year.

Debts/Liabilities: What the firm owes or its obligations, including its promises or obligations to provide a product or service in the future.

Depreciation: The wear and tear on some assets (machinery, tools, furniture, etc.), which are used over the long term.

Dividends: Earnings distributed to shareholders.

Expenses: Using assets to generate a profit or to incur new liabilities.

Fixed Asset: property which cannot easily be converted into cash (land, buildings, machinery, etc.).

Income/Profit: Revenue – Expenses = Income/Profit (when spending is less than money generated/cost of goods sold).

Loss: Revenue – Expenses = Loss (when spending is more than money generated).

Margins: Difference in cost and desired selling price.

Net Profit/Net Earnings/Bottom Line: How much money the company actually earned or lost during an accounting period.

Net Worth: What the company owns minus what it owes

Owner's Equity/Shareholder's Equity/Stockholder's Equity: Money that would be left if a company sold all of its assets and paid off all of its liabilities.

Revenue: Money generated from sale of goods/use of services

Shareholders/Stockholders: The owners of shares/shares and thus part owners of a corporation.

FINANCIAL STATEMENTS

The three most commonly used financial statements are The Income Statement, The Balance Sheet and The Statement of Cash Flows:

An Income Statement measures performance over a specific period of time, often a year. It is also called the P&L – profit and loss statement. An income statement is a report that shows how much revenue a company earned over a specific time period (usually for a year or some portion of a year). It also shows the costs and expenses associated with earning that revenue.

A Balance Sheet documents what the firm owns and how it is financed. It provides detailed information about a company's assets, liabilities, and shareholders' equity. It is a snapshot of the firm's relative strength at a point in time.

A Statement of Cash Flows explains how a company obtained and used cash during an accounting period. Cash transactions are classified as both cash flows from operating (cash generated from the firm's normal activities in producing and selling goods and services), investing and financing activities. Cash may be money or its equivalents. This report is important because a company needs to have enough cash on hand to pay its expenses and purchase assets.

No one financial statement tells the complete story. However, when combined, The Income Statement, The Balance Sheet, and The Statement of Cash Flows provide very powerful information for decision makers including owners, investors, and the competition. All companies operating in the United States, foreign and domestic, are required to file registration statements, periodic reports, and other forms to the US Securities and Exchange Commission (SEC). Anyone can access and download this information for free through EDGAR, the SEC's Electronic Data Gathering, Analysis, and Retrieval system (United States Securities Exchange Commission, n.d.). However, these filings are lagging indicators of performance and conditions can and do change. Companies are required to disclose their accounting policies and practices. Most companies use Generally Accepted Accounting Principles (GAAP).

CAVEATS ABOUT FINANCIAL RATIOS

Financial ratios fall into several categories: profitability, liquidity, activity, and leverage (Demonstrating Value, 2013). Once the financial statements have been developed, a quantitative analysis on the numbers can be used to determine how well the company is doing and how well it is doing in comparison to its closest rivals in the industry. It is important to note there are usually two sides to the story of any ratio. Thus, it is important to examine a company's performance over time rather than a single period. For ratios to be useful and meaningful, they must be:

- Calculated using reliable, accurate financial information.

- Calculated consistently from period to period.

- Viewed both at a single point in time and over time. (Numbers from the previous period are used as starting points of the comparison.)

- Linked to objectives.

- Compared to other companies in the industry. (Refer to Standard & Poor's Financial Services and the Risk Management Association for industry averages.)

- Carefully interpreted in the proper context, considering how other important factors impact performance.

Throughout this book, inconsistencies in terms used in the strategic management process have been noted. As pointed out by Mankin and Jewell (2014), although it would be reasonable to assume that once some-one learns a financial ratio he/she can apply that ratio in a variety of situations with little potential for error or confusion. However, that is not the case. There are minor variations in financial ratio formulas and names. Notwithstanding, this is a good lesson to learn. Understand that not all companies will use the same terminology (names and titles for financial ratios) in their financial statements. As with other information, you should confirm how your company computes and interprets the ratios. The preferred use should be the same within the company and hopefully the industry.

KEY FINANCIAL RATIOS FOR ANALYZING A COMPANY MS USED IN THE STRATEGIC MA

Although there is inconsistency in the terminology, we will discuss profitability, liquidity, and leverage ratio as set forth by Lan (2012). Profitability ratios are used to assess a business's ability to generate revenue compared to its expenses during a specific period of time. Profitability ratios are arguably the most widely used ratios in investment analysis.

Gross Profit Margin

It is an indication of the total margin available to cover operating expenses and yield a profit. Gross profit margin is calculated by dividing gross income (revenue less cost of goods sold) by net revenue (gross income ÷ net revenue). The ratio reflects pricing decisions and product costs. For most firms, gross profit margin suffers as competition increases. A low gross profit margin could mean the company is paying too much for its products or services or setting selling prices too low (or giving away too much through sales discounts or promotions). A low margin could also signal inefficiencies in manufacturing or service delivery.

Operating Profit Margin

An indication of the firm's profitability from current operations without regard to the interest charges accruing from the capital structure. Same as Return on Sales. Increasing operating margin is generally seen as a good sign. Operating profit margin is calculated by dividing operating income (gross income minus operating expenses) by net revenue (operating income ÷ net revenue). Operating expenses include costs such as administrative overhead and other costs that cannot be attributed to single product units. A 10% return on sales means that $.10 of each sales dollar remains after all expenses are paid.

Net Profit Margin

It compares a company's net income to its net revenue. This ratio is calculated by dividing net income by net revenue (net income ÷ net revenue). Same as net Return on Sales.

Earnings Before Interest and Taxes (EBIT)

This shows operating profit minus financing costs and income taxes. This ratio is calculated by adding net income, income taxes, and interest expense (net income + income taxes + interest expense). Firms have different debt and cost structures and may be affected by different tax laws (federal, state, local, and/or foreign). By factoring out these variables, you can see how efficient a firm is relative to its competitors.

Earnings per Share (EPS)

This shows how much shareholders would receive for each share of stock they own if the company distributed all of its net income for the period. This ratio is calculated by dividing net income by the average number of outstanding shares (net income ÷ average outstanding common shares). Be careful not to confuse shares issued and shares outstanding. Shares issued are the number of shares a company has offered for sale. Conversely, shares outstanding are the number of shares actually purchased and owned by shareholders.

Return on Assets (ROA)

ROA measures how efficiently a firm utilizes its assets. This ratio is calculated by dividing net income by total assets (net income ÷ total assets). ROA can also be calculated using EBIT divided by total assets (EBIT ÷ total assets) based on pretax and pre-interest earnings. A high ratio reflects effective utilization of assets to generate profit.

Return on Equity (ROE)

While ROA measures net income, ROE measures net income less preferred dividends against total shareholder's equity. This ratio is calculated by dividing net income by shareholder's equity (net income ÷ total shareholder equity). This ratio measures the level of income attributed to shareholders against the investment that shareholders put into the firm. It considers the amount of debt, or financial leverage, a firm uses. Financial leverage magnifies the impact of earnings on ROE in both good and bad years. If there are large discrepancies between the ROA and ROE, the firm may be incorporating a large amount of debt.

Liquidity Ratios

Liquidity ratios measure a firm's ability to meet its short-term obligations. The level of liquidity needed varies from industry to industry. Certain industries are more cash-intensive than others are.

Current Ratio

This measures a company's current assets against its current liabilities. The current ratio indicates if the company can pay off its short-term liabilities in an emergency by liquidating its current assets. This ratio is calculated by dividing current assets by current liabilities (current assets ÷ current liabilities). A low current ratio indicates that a firm may have a hard time paying their current liabilities in the short run and deserves further investigation. A current ratio under 1.00x, for example, means that even if the company liquidates all of its current assets, it would be unable to cover its current liabilities. A current ratio that is too high, however, may indicate that the company is carrying too much inventory, allowing accounts receivables to balloon with lax payment collection standards or simply holding too much in cash.

Quick Ratio

This measures the firm's ability to pay off short-term obligations without selling its inventories. This ratio is calculated by adding cash, cash equivalents, short-term investments and current receivables together and then dividing them by current liabilities (cash + cash equivalents + short-term investments + accounts receivable ÷ current liabilities). If the company needs to quickly liquidate inventory, the inventory it is carrying may be worth less than the inventory figure shown in its financial statements if the value of assets have gone down. The market will determine value/worth.

Activity Ratios

These are used to measure how efficiently a company utilizes its assets. The ratios provide investors with an idea of the overall operational performance of a firm. Activity ratios measure the rate at which the company is turning over its assets or liabilities. In other words, they present how many times per year inventory is replenished or receivables are collected.

Inventory Turnover

This is calculated by dividing the cost of goods sold by average inventory (cost of goods sold ÷ average inventory). A higher turnover than the industry average means that inventory is sold at a faster rate, signaling inventory management effectiveness. Additionally, a high inventory turnover rate means less company resources are tied up in inventory.

Asset Turnover Ratio

This measures how efficiently a company uses its total assets to generate revenues. The asset turnover ratio is calculated by dividing net revenues divided by average total assets (net revenues ÷ average total assets). A low asset turnover ratio may mean that the firm is inefficient in its use of its assets or that it is operating in a capital-intensive environment. Additionally, it may point to a strategic choice by management to use a more capital-intensive (as opposed to a more labor-intensive) approach.

Leverage Ratios

Leverage ratios measure a company's ability to meet its longer-term obligations. Analysis of leverage ratios provides insight into a company's capital structure as well as the level of financial leverage a firm is using. Some leverage ratios allow investors to see whether a firm has adequate cash flows to consistently pay interest payments and other fixed charges. If a company does not have enough cash flows, the firm is most likely overburdened with debt and bondholders may force the company into default.

Debt-to-Assets Ratio

This measures the extent to which borrowed money has been used to finance the firm's operations. This ratio is calculated by dividing total liabilities by total assets (total liabilities ÷ total assets). A high number means the firm is using a larger amount of financial leverage, which increases its financial risk in the form of fixed interest payments.

Debt-to-Equity Ratio

This measures the amount of debt capital a firm uses compared to the amount of equity capital it uses. This ratio is calculated by dividing total debt by total shareholder's equity (total debt ÷ total shareholder's equity). A ratio of 1.00 × indicates that the firm uses the same amount of debt as equity and means that creditors have claim to all assets, leaving nothing for shareholders in the event of a theoretical liquidation.

Long-term Debt to Equity Ratio

This measures the balance between debt and equity in the firm's long-term capital structure. This ratio is calculated by dividing long-term debt by total assets (long-term debt ÷ total shareholders' equity). The higher the figure, the more degree of risk a company has, as it must be able to cover both principal and interest on its debts/liabilities.

Interest Coverage Ratio

This measures a company's cash flows generated compared to its interest payments. This ratio is calculated by dividing EBIT by interest payments (EBIT (earnings before interest and taxes) ÷ interest payments. The higher the figure, the better the company is at generating earnings compared to its interest obligations.

ADDITIONAL TOOLS

Comparing ratios of firms within a strategic group informs the problem solver on where operational issues can be found and provides a rationale for determining the best approach to address those issues. It is beyond the scope of this book to show all planning tools that may be used in the implementation planning process. Many experts have put videos and blogs online that explain these and other tools. You can find them by searching YouTube or Googling "project management tools."

11

THE ART OF GAINING COMMITMENT
BY RAISING THE STAKES

Recall, in business, a stake represents an interest in outcomes. Have you heard the saying, "when the stakes are high," which signals that the decisions under consideration have significant consequences? Most of the decisions we make every day are subconscious. However, when you understand the implications and determine that the outcomes matter, you consider your thoughts and actions.

A meeting to present an implementation plan has two major aims: to get the plan accepted and to get the decision makers to disclose any issues they have with the plan that would keep the plan from being implemented as proposed. Step 8 of implementation planning involves presenting the draft of the plan to the decision makers for input and commitment. Adjusting as necessary; clearly communicating the process and procedures that went into the development of the draft and the future steps to finalize the plan. Moreover, Chapter 5 in Part I included a section on overcoming resistance, particularly when dealing with parties with opposing views and interests. Three outcomes were mentioned that could help you address stakeholder concerns:

1) gaining their cooperation (play an active role as needed);

2) gaining their agreement to not challenge the plan if cooperation is not needed or possible; and

3) overcoming challenges to the perceived pitfalls or actions that are deemed to negatively impact stakeholder interest(s).

Addressing these three concerns improves the likelihood that the implementation plan will be understood, valued, and approved. The success of any strategy lies in the commitment of the organization and of the people managing the process. By commitment, I mean the willingness to provide the support needed for a strategy to be effective. If you know your stakeholders well, you will know their priorities and what information they likely need to know to be convinced that change must happen and to commit to the success of the strategy. Whether through written communications, web conferencing or face-to-face or virtual meetings; storytelling, a functional analysis, examples, templates, visuals, an Appendix, and a summary handout can help gain their commitment.

WRITTEN COMMUNICATIONS

Guffey and Loewy (2018) recommend a recursive 3-x-3 writing process to communicate ideas to stakeholders in business letters, memos, and reports. They suggested the writer(s) begin with pre-writing ideas in their mind or brainwriting on paper to adapt the message to primary or the intended stakeholder *and* secondary stakeholder(s) who are likely to read the message in anticipation of both of their responses. They assert that readers will want to know "what is in it [the message] for them" or how a strategy will affect their outcomes and thus writers should write with a "you" or receiver focus. In other words, instead of focusing on your needs, focus on what the stakeholders might need or want. Then, they suggest writers craft a first draft based on what they know or find in their research, and lastly, revise the work continually for clarity to ensure the message would likely accomplish their objectives. This approach of carefully thinking about the primary and secondary audiences and anticipating how they might react to a message is valid irrespective of communicating in writing or conversations. Recall that stakeholders may have power to influence your organization's outcomes either positively or negatively. Thus, supplying adequate background information can enhance the likelihood that you secure their cooperation.

Here are some tips for good writing, including some by a master linguist, Steven Pinker (2016) that can be adapted and also applied to storytelling:

Be visual and conversational. Be concrete; ensure your stakeholders understand and stop trying to impress.

Beware "the curse of knowledge." Have someone read your report or listen to your story and tell you if it makes sense. Don't trust yourself to ensure that it does.

Don't bury the lead. Clarity beats suspense. If they don't know what your story is about they can't follow along.

You don't have to play by the rules of grammar but try. In written reports, at least use the spellcheck and grammar function in your word processing software. In oral reports or presentations, be careful to refer to the stakeholders by name or roles, and do not use catch-all phrases such as "stakeholders" or "you guys."

Read Read Read. There is too much information about an industry, company, strategy, product, or service, etc. to learn everything from one book. Never stop learning.

WEB CONFERENCING

When the message is straightforward, communication is mostly one-way, and there is a minimal expectation of resistance, a web conference via the telephone using a passcode will usually suffice. Schedule the call when most contributors are available to attend, send out an agenda prior to the call, use conferencing technology that allows you to present visuals to explain details, often in an approved template, encourage participants to submit questions prior to, during, and after the call, and send out the promised material/content and a recording of the session within seven business days.

FACE-TO-FACE AND VIRTUAL MEETINGS

When the stakes are higher, it is necessary to get people around the table. A meeting provides an opportunity for the contributors with expertise to converse, share stories, observe body language, look their audience in the eye, and ask questions in real time. A meeting can be informal or formal. An informal meeting may be impromptu or scheduled. It may be held in an office, on the golf course, over a meal, and virtually, etc. The attendees are problem solvers who have a need to discuss topics for clarity, updates, reporting out, etc. While an informal meeting usually does not have a written agenda, there are usually some topics that need to be covered. It is best practice for all parties to know what those topics are in advance. However, with an impromptu meeting that may not be possible and therefore some details may not be covered as thoroughly as necessary. Thus, many impromptu meetings require a follow-up meeting. Many informal meetings serve as a prelude to an upcoming formal meeting. It is often during these informal meetings where favors for assistance are called in and the details are worked out.

However, face-to-face meetings with all of the decision makers regarding the formulation of a strategy or implementation of your strategic plan should be formal. Below are some considerations to set up your meeting successfully:

- *Travel.* If it is necessary to bring people from different locations together for an in-person meeting, then follow company policies, reflect your company well, and dress for success (just in case you encounter another thinking strategist along on your way, your luggage is delayed, or you need to be ready to conduct business as soon as you arrive), and treat support staff well (e.g., tips and other hospitality courtesies).

- *Space.* A formal meeting is usually held in a space that is designed for meetings or collaboration among people who are directly involved in the strategy making process or a specific phase in the process. A U-shaped arrangement allows interactions and the ability for members to see each other and possibly make eye contact.

- *Notice.* The participants should know in advance that a meeting will take place at a given time and location and thus should be able to limit interruptions or distractions.

- *Frequency.* Formal meetings may be scheduled weekly, monthly, or over a period of days. Weekly and monthly meetings are used to update participants. Meetings held over a period of days are often planning meetings that will later be followed up with weekly or monthly meetings.

- *Length*. The time set aside for a weekly or monthly meeting should be limited to less than 90 minutes to accommodate differences in attention spans. Meetings that run too long run the risk of participants becoming distracted thinking about tasks related to their roles or anticipated activities after the meeting.

- *Refreshments*. A meeting planned for over 90 minutes should include a break and snacks as incentives for attendance and staying until the meeting is adjourned.

- *Materials*. Presentation software such as PowerPoint, Prezi, and Smart-Draw can help to share information easily. Flip charts or dry-erase boards are helpful in moving through information in real time. These tools and other meeting logistics should be communicated prior to the meeting.

- *Agenda*. A written agenda serves as a timekeeper during formal meetings. It identifies the topics that are planned to be covered and is often shared prior to the meeting. This simple act helps to aid participants to be prepared to discuss thoughtfully the topics listed and enables them to contribute to the process within the allotted time. When key topics are missing, participants can request that those topics be added to the agenda.

- *Reminders*. Send reminders via calendars and emails. This courtesy can ensure that people arrive at the meeting on time.

- *Follow-up*. If there are no expectations for follow-up, participants may deem the meeting as unnecessary or unproductive. Thus, clearly stating the purpose of the meeting tends to result in better outcomes. Likewise, minutes with action items and planned dates should be shared expeditiously while the meeting is fresh in the minds of the participants. Meeting minutes should be distributed at least three days prior to the deadline of the last action item. Members should expect to report out on their activities in the next meeting or in a written report. It may also be customary for participants to send out points that were not covered or unclear after the meeting.

Virtual meetings with the decision makers should also be formal. While travel, space, and refreshments are inapplicable, the other considerations are relevant including breaks. Additionally, efforts should be made to ensure that the video teleconferencing software is able to handle the organization's need for collaboration and privacy.

PRESENTING THE MEETING CONTENT

Exchanging information is the primary reason meetings are held. Reporting out, an internal tracking process that allows the person who is responsible for an activity to inform others of the progress made to date is often an important part of the meeting. The "report" can be verbal (face-to-face, in a meeting, etc.) or written and distributed via hand or an electronic source. It can be brief or lengthy, but the report must be detailed enough so that other members of the team – whether present or absent – will know the status of an activity at a certain point in time. Remember, in cases when you have distributed a report beforehand, the attendees are supposed to have read your report, and thus there is no need to belabor every single point during your talk. Instead, point out the unresolved issues that need to be finalized or those things that need to be acted upon. However, if it is evident that they have not read your report, as expected, then you will need to be more detailed in your discussion of the issues.

VALUE OF STORYTELLING AND USE OF EXAMPLES

Good stories are based on real problems. Storytelling is an art in itself. The story has to be told in a logical way that the stakeholders will come to a particular conclusion without the storyteller having to explicitly make a point or recommendation. The end is obvious because of your ability to connect the dots that matter to the audience. A good story will help stakeholders understand how the problem impacts them or others that contribute to their success. When introducing a problem, the end result is to gain a commitment *to do something* about the problem. When discussing a solution to the problem, the end result is to gain a commitment to take your specific recommendation about how to resolve it. That *something* may be to ignore the problem or not to make any changes at this time. However, the decision to do nothing is a decision.

A really good business problem story creates lasting images and invokes fear, anxiety, and pain. They end with a notion that with a good strategy whatever caused those images and emotions can be reduced if not eliminated. If the audience leaves without experiencing some emotional connection, the wrong story was told, or the wrong people were in the room. When stakeholders are likely to agree with your recommendations or findings, the meeting in which you present your ideas will most likely go well and end relatively quickly without much dissent. However, when the stakeholders are likely to not be swayed by your findings, you must prepare to persuade them to act with convincing evidence. Good storytelling takes practice. Never tell your story to decision makers without practicing how you want it to flow – preferably multiple times.

Examples are very useful in gaining alignment. Managers are expected to lead by example, set an example, and provide examples. Trent North, in Forensic Leadership: Changing the Culture of a Nation, defined forensics as skills in investigating and establishing facts for evidence at the smallest or most simplistic level possible (North, 2012). It requires one to focus on the smaller fragments of an organization to get to the underlying causes or truths. North provides an example of forensic leadership through setting expectations about the cleanliness of the building he oversaw as principal. North wrote:

> I expected the building to be clean and remain clean. I could not simply tell the custodian that without specifically conveying my expectations. For me to tell the head custodian, "I want my building to be clean" [but] not provide training and inspect what I expected would not yield the results that I wanted. I worked with my custodians on how to clean a bathroom and how to maintain that level of cleanliness which required that I know how to clean a bathroom.

North continued to work alongside his staff. In doing so and in asking the right questions, he was able to learn more about their skills and thus be more exact in stating his expectations. North conveys that when he learned that one of the contributors could paint, he informed the supervisory staff that he expected to see marks put on the wall by a child removed within 24 hours. The staff complied and knew the request was based on a perceived strength and therefore not an unreasonable request. According to North, two years later he received compliments that the "building still looked brand new." North, as an administrator, led by example and set the example. Thus, he raised the stakes for everyone.

VALUE OF A SUPPORTING FUNCTIONAL ANALYSIS

When problem solvers come up with ideas for strategies they would like to recommend, they tend to envision the potential outcomes of each option. Anticipating some of the concerns that the decision makers may bring up is not uncommon. Moreover, decision makers and problem solvers tend to rely on one tool: the one they know best. Thus, it is a good idea to follow-up the decision analysis with a functional analysis, a tool that can provide additional support for your final decision.

Here, a functional analysis is not an analysis of your functional areas. Rather here, a functional analysis is an analysis that is commonly used *within* one of the company's functional areas that can support or provide further insights regarding how the final decision can be implemented. Someone with a financial background may use or expect financial ratios or projections to show expected returns. A marketing expert may rely on the four P's: price, product, promotion, and place to meet customer need or demand. An operations expert may ask that the decision makers consider production schedules to show that the firm is more than capable of handling the new opportunities. Which functional analyses are needed is based on the competencies and interests of the stakeholders? Those that are given are usually based on the competencies and interests of the presenters.

The key here is not to talk in generalities. Be as detail oriented as possible. Show strong visuals that paint a clear picture of what can be done and what steps have already been taken to determine that the option chosen was the best (viable and attainable). Here may be a point when you can show how your proposed strategy compares – and hopefully is expected to outperform – your competitors.

When considering functional analyses, consider those that show:

- staffing requirements (number of people available) have been considered;

- people who are involved are highly competent;

- money is there to handle the costs of implementing the strategy;

- technology is available or in place for improved effectiveness and efficiency; and

- incentives are in place to bring people on board.

VALUE OF VISUAL REPRESENTATIONS

If you can communicate your message clearly in a sentence or statement, that is the easiest way to make a point. However, visuals help to make points clear and organized. Duquia, Bastos, Bonamigo, González-Chica, and Martínez-Mesa (2014) emphasized that visuals should be understandable without the need to be explained by a presenter or the need to read the text to which they refer. Following are six steps to create effective visuals:

1. Check the quality/accuracy of the data.

2. Outline the story you want to tell a specific stakeholder.

3. Choose the right visuals for that story.

4. Use a consistent background and include an insightful title, column/row headings, legend to ensure proper identification of the data, etc.

5. Provide the source of the data.

6. Customize with the company's logo and slogan.

To evaluate the effectiveness of your visual, determine- Is the visual self-explanatory? Are the values presented in a standard or consistent format? Does it tell the story you want to tell? If not, make these corrections before presenting it to the decision makers.

Table 35 reveals that visuals serve different purposes. The basic visual for displaying information, particularly when you want to share specific numbers with the stakeholder(s) is a table. When asked to create a table, remember a row is horizontal display of information in cells. A column is a verticaldisplay of information in cells. In a contingency table, the information inthe cells of a row is contingent on the information in the column heading.Likewise, the information in the 20 cells of the 5 columns is contingent

Table 35. Visuals in Storytelling.

Use of Visuals in Storytelling	
Purpose	Visual
To show exact values	Table
To depict relationships through shapes	Chart or graph
To compare a part to the whole	Pie chart
To compare items over time	Bar graph
To show frequency or distribution	Bar graph/line graph
To show correlations	Bar graph/line graph/dot chart (scatterplot)
To show overlap among data	Venn diagram
To show something or someone in action	Photograph
To show hierarchy	Organizational chart
To show details that have not been captured in photos	Drawing
To show branding or identity	Logo
To show facilities	Site visit or photos
To show locations	Map
To show a product	Demonstration
To show process or progress	Workflow diagram

onthe information in the 4 row headings. If there are no headings, then thein-formation is simply a list formatted as a table. Software can transform a table into graphs and charts. Graphs are more memorable and can help to tell a more visually compelling story than tables. Pictures and drawings also tell a great story when images rather than numbers are desired, but nothing is more effective than a product demonstration.

VALUE OF AN APPENDIX AND SUMMARY HANDOUTS

Information that is crucial to the decision that is under consideration goes into the body of the report. Supplemental information should be included in an Appendix:

- A copy of the instrument used to collect data.

- Additional information that supports the outcomes.

- Information that refutes the outcomes.

- Additional subplans.

- Previous reports.

- Citations and sources.

Key points that you want stakeholders to remember should be captured in a professionally developed summary handout. I recommend that the summary is one-page front and back (bullets and short narrative or key visuals that you want them to consider after the meeting- this may include information that was not covered at the meeting). Additionally, the handout can suggest additional sources of information. It should always include your contact information. The agenda or a printout of your presentation slides does not suffice as a summary handout. An agenda can be a separate handout. You can offer to send the slides later, but slides are not intended to capture the thought process that a narrative would provide. Thus, sending them may not yield the desired results.

Lastly, the summary should be *for* the stakeholder, not *about* the stakeholder. Only information that the stakeholder is unlikely to know should be included. For example, including their mission statement shows you did your homework, but no doubt they did not attend the meeting to learn their mission statement. On the other hand, if you are showing them why the mission statement needs to be changed to reflect their current operations, then it is absolutely necessary.

VALUE OF CITATIONS AND SOURCES

Including the information that is needed to provide a complete picture makes it easier to gain alignment. Unless you have firsthand knowledge, you should provide sources of the information. Adding sources makes you a more credible presenter and shows that you have done your research.

As mentioned in Chapter 1 in Part II, including the views of those with whom you disagree also adds to your credibility and shows you have considered alternative perspectives. The use of verbs in your story or report indicates whether you agree or disagree with a source. When presenters or storytellers are making a neutral point, verbs such as says, mentions, notes, or wrote are used. However, when they disagree with something, they tend to distance themselves from the information through such verbs as suggests, claims, and alleges.

All of these resources allow the thinking strategist to tell a convincing story that will move the decision makers to engage in the meeting and ultimately to act. Just remember that a simple straightforward story with the desired outcome is easier to gain commitment than a complicated one. Experiment with each resource and eliminate those things that only complicate the story (use your Appendix wisely). In the end, you will have the approval you need to move forward with implementing the plan, or the feedback you need to determine if improvements to the plan are needed.

12

STRATEGIC COMMUNICATIONS

Throughout the strategic management process, strategic communications is an important activity that meshes the function of internal communications and customer-facing functions (such as customer service, advertising publicity, public relations, media relations, and branding) into one complementary package. As a business function or department, this group has the responsibility of determining what should be communicated, how, how often, when, and where. The goal of strategic communications is to promote engagement and contributions in the process across the board, including promoting products and services, strategically sharing outcomes with key stakeholders, and celebrating wins, even the small ones. While every individual in the organization engages in strategic communications, when adding to this function, the thinking strategist becomes an asset by communicating information judiciously and effectively and ensuring that the diversity of thought that is often valued is not lost, but captured in the message.

MESSAGING

In order to achieve impact worthy of a seat at the table, your presence within your firm should be felt. To appreciate your worth, colleagues throughout the organization will have to see how and why your contributions matter to their success and the success of the firm. This is best achieved through effective communications. Purposefully sending communications to an intended audience is the core of strategic communication. When it comes to communication, not only do problem solvers and contributors need to be able to effectively explain the value of their recommendations to their colleagues and decision makers, but decision makers at multiple levels must also be able to then explain the value of the approved strategies to the decision maker at the next level.

Messaging should be considered in oral or written communication, as well as body language and tone. In cases of important communications, not only should a problem solver consider how the message may be received by the intended audience, but he or she can practice the delivery to be effective in real time.

Here, I will give you three points of caution.

1) *Assume that your message could be misconstrued.* For example, you send a message "Dinner is for 6." Some might interpret that message to mean 6 people while others might interpret the message as dinner will take place at 6 pm. Alternatively, you include titles in your email signature, but fail to include the dates that you held the position(s). Some stakeholders might seek to engage you rather than the person who currently holds the position. Therefore, be thorough in your statements. When necessary ask for an assurance of understanding and include the need for/your planned expected follow-up.

2) *Assume that the communication will be shared with someone who was not the intended audience (by forwarding or including in a response, etc.).* In written communications, draft with an extended audience in mind. Do not include statements that you would not want to be shared with others beyond your intended audience, and explicitly point out why the message was sent to those who were intended to receive the message. The same applies to oral communications; others may not uphold your confidence.

3) *Assume that your messaging signals company values to stakeholders.* Imagine you are a stakeholder seeking to join a firm or to do business with a firm- the company's communications can provide the insights needed for a stakeholder to decide about whether or not to engage. Thus, the messaging really matters in making the right impression on others.

COMMUNICATION FUNCTIONS

Aligning communication functions is essential to ensure stakeholders receive consistent messages. Optimal outcomes require Research & Development, Marketing, and Strategic Communications to work together from conception to placement of products and services. Common functions include:

- *Internal communications.* Efforts to present information in ways that other contributors within the company can use it to be successful in their roles.

- *Advertising.* Efforts to promote a company, product, or service to attract buyers.

- *Publicity.* Attention given to a company, contributor, product, or service by the media.

- *Public relations.* Efforts to influence the perception that stakeholders have about a company, contributor, product, or service.

- *Media relations.* Efforts to establish relationships with news outlets for favorable coverage/publicity.

- *Branding.* Efforts to establish a unique identity for a company, contributor, product, or service.

- *Customer service.* Efforts to assist buyers with the purchase, delivery, and use of a product or service.

- *Social media.* Efforts to engage directly with the stakeholders through an official public account via the Internet.

An organizational structure that has these functions reporting to the same executive helps to ensure that they are talking to each other in the decision making process.

THE PROCESS

Fig. 33 outlines a strategic approach to communicating with stakeholders.

Fig. 33. The Strategic Communication Process.

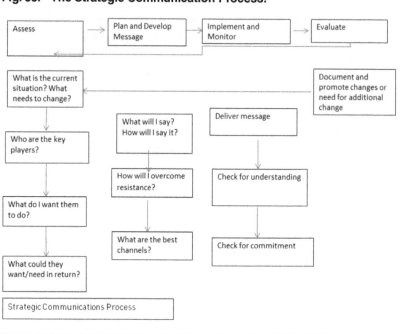

KISS THE MESSAGE

A KISS approach to strategic communication is an attempt to simplify the message and thus make it easier to understand what is happening in a situation. KISS, which is an acronym for K.eep I.t S.hort or S.imple or K.eep I.t S.imple and S.traightforward, emphasizes succinct oral and written communication between the team and with stakeholders. This approach promotes the use of visuals (i.e., process maps) rather than long and/or narrative explanations. Moreover, a KISS approach eases some of the tension that may accompany uncertainty and ambiguity in the change process.

PROCESS MAPPING AND MODELING

At times, it is necessary to share a thinking process with others. Doing so provides direction so we do not lose our way on what some may consider a complicated way of doing things. Also, by sharing the process, we can expect milestones for measuring success. For example, in onboarding new hires, showing them how things are done within an organization helps to determine how things are handled in this organization as opposed to how something may have been done in other companies or situations.

These activities can be accomplished through business process mapping and business process modeling. When problem solving, having a road map helps to ensure that everyone knows what to expect and where potential problems may be encountered. Business process mapping shows how work is currently done. Business process modeling shows how work is currently done and highlights inefficiencies and bottlenecks that constrain the system. Additionally, when compliance is of concern, documenting how things are done helps to ensure that everything is in order.

JUST IN TIME COMMUNICATION

Having the right information at your fingertips is important. You cannot expect to know everything about every topic. However, you can be adept at knowing where to find what you need to know quickly, especially when timely decisions must be made, or it is clear that not all information that needs to be taken into consideration has been relayed to the decision makers.

The ability to quickly sort through thousands of documents, emails (archive all important communications on your work and personal smart devices), social media pages, Internet files, etc. AND cite *when* that information was shared and *by and with whom* provides you with an edge. You can become that go-to person that can be relied on to ensure relevant data is available.

Organize information in folders according to personal or business. Include a folder for major topics/activities in your business map. Identify and share information about effective file sharing and online organization tools.

CELEBRATIONS AND COMMITMENTS

Organizations that regard the strategic management process as an integral part of their problem solving efforts are equipped to work with various stakeholders to achieve goals. To that end, thinking strategists should seriously consider how best to solve problems and ensure that everyone in the organization has a good understanding of the processes that problem solvers and contributors need to make better decisions and to critically engage the strategic management process. You should intentionally strive to enhance your worth by linking with others with similar goals and interests, as well as those from diverse backgrounds and experience levels that can help you solve problems better and faster. "Meet" with them regularly, swap advice, and remember the lessons learned when you take your place at the table.

For Your Toolbox

Throughout this textbook, you have been asked to consider how the content applies to your ability to be a trusted, intuitive, and competent team player (i.e., a thinking strategist). Give your toolbox a title that reflects who you are. Update the content as you further evolve. Include both your successes and failures. One day you may decide to publish the toolbox for other thinking strategists.

Don't just dream about success – work for it. Intelligence, past experiences, connections, etc., are barometers of your potential for success. While such barometers are useful in helping you become better at what you want to achieve, in order to achieve genuine long-term success and authentic recognition for being an expert, you cannot rely on intelligence, past experiences, and connections. You must have the knowledge, skills, and abilities that others can depend on for improved performance. You must view failure as an opportunity and not an end. Publicly embrace it as such and others will know you are human, just like them. You can overcome any failure by analyzing what happened and identifying a new choice that is better suited given what you learn.

The Thinking Strategist is a powerful tool in the hands of an ambitious and skilled problem solver. Don't forget to celebrate small wins along the way to keep the momentum going. While a huge announcement that a strategy will launch is welcome, providing celebratory feedback to those doing the work as the process unfolds signifies a respect for the work and helps contributors to own their efforts. Celebrate, but only for a day. Then, it is time to go back to informing and influencing decision making and the strategic management process with timely, fact-based insights and knowledge. As Fig. 4 implies, you can make success happen! Be a Thinking Strategist.

APPENDIX

Appendix 1. Comparison of Firm Relative Strength Template

	Firm X (Your Firm Here)	Firm A	Firm B	Firm C	Firm D	Relative Strength (Based on Resources)
Resource 1						
Resource 2						
Resource 3						
Constraint 1						
Constraint 2						
Constraint 3						

Appendix 2. Analyzing Undesirable Effects Template

What Should Be Happening	Undesirable Effects	Where is the UDE Visible to Stakeholder(s)?	Stakeholder Type	Where is the Presumed Solution (s)?
Desired outcome	DDE 1	Stakeholder	I or E	Functional area
Desired outcome	UDE 2	Stakeholder	I or E	Functional area
Desired outcome	UDE 3	Stakeholder	I or E	Functional area
Desired outcome	UDE 4	Stakeholder	I or E	Functional area

Appendix 3.   Decision Matrix

	A		B		C		D	
Decision Matrix								
Current Reality:								
Decision Analysis Statement:								
	A		**B**		**C**		**D**	
Strategy-based objectives	WT	SC	WT SC	SC	WT SC	SC	WT SC	SC	WT SC

Total weighted scores

Final decision:
Strategic options legend:

Appendix 4.   Implementation Plan or Subplan Components and Responsibility List Template

Implementation Plan Components and Responsibility List

Plan Statement:
Objective 1: Talent -
Objective 2: Time -
Objective 3: Budget -

Component/tactic/activity	Who	Strategic Options

Strategic options legend:

Appendix 5. Potential Problem Avoidance Analysis-Potential Problems Accepted Risk Template

Potential Problem Avoidance Analysis			
Potential Problem Avoidance Statement:			
Potential Problems	**Probability**	**Seriousness**	**Accepted Risk**

Appendix 6. Potential Problem Avoidance Analysis-Likely Causes of Potential Problem Template

Potential Problem Avoidance Analysis: Likely Causes of Potential Problem A						
Potential Problem Avoidance Statement:						
A	**Potential Problem:**	**P M**	**S H**	**Probability**	**Seriousness**	**Accepted Risk**
Likely Causes						

Appendix 7.   Potential Problem Avoidance Analysis Contingency-Planning for Potential Problem-Template

Potential Problem Avoidance Analysis: Contingency Planning for Potential Problem			
Potential Problem Avoidance Statement			
A	**Potential Problem**	**P**	**S**
Likely Causes	Preventive Actions	Who	RP
Contingent Action:	Triggers: PT: RT:	Who	

Appendix 8.   Team Contribution Worksheet

Team Contribution Worksheet					
Plan Statement: Objective 1: Talent Objective 2: Time Objective 3: Budget					
Tactic	**Who**	**Planned Date**	**Actual Date**	**Cause of Deviation**	**Information Source**

Appendix 9.   Individual Contribution Worksheet

Individual Contribution Worksheet

Your Name
Your Role (Area of Expertise)

Tactic	Volunteered Y or N	Planned Date	Actual Date	Cause of Deviation	Information Source	Additional Notes

Appendix 10.   Plan Objective Test for Talent Template

Plan Objective Test
Objective 1

Plan Statement:
Objective 1: Talent

Component/Tactic/Activity	Who	Strategic Options

Legend for strategic options

Appendix 11. Plan Objective Test for Time Template

Plan Objective Test
Objective 2

Plan Statement:
Objective 2: Time

Time Period	Activity Planned		Activity Actual		Cause of Deviation? Cost Saved or Incurred
	Start	Finish	Start	Finish	

Legends for Implementation Planning:
Time Period Legend:
I = First two weeks of the month
II = Second two weeks of the month
Component Legend:
Subcomponent Legend:

Appendix 12. Plan Objective Test Budget Template

Plan Objective Test
Objective 3

Plan Statement:
Objective 3
Cost Projections

Components and Subcomponents	Projected Cost	Total Remaining	Actual Cost	Cause of Deviation

❏ Under budget substantially
❏ Over budget
❏ Over budget substantially

Included are all components in the proposed strategy that will require money from the budget. Components that are most vital to plan success are listed first.

Appendix 13. Worksheet for Smart Objectives-Based Progress Report for College Teams

Team#:
Company Researched#:
S.M.A.R.T Objectives-Based Progress Report
Teem Members end Roles:

Kay Result Area	Due Date	Total Pts. Possible	Objective	Performance	Commentary on Feedback	Corrective Actions

Total
Points

Appendix 14. Worksheet for Driving Forces Analysis Template

Forces Driving Industry Competition and Profit Analysis

Industry_____SIC Code_____ Industry Size_____
Products or Services Offered:_____Market share_____ Strategy Type_____
Assessment of Forces

   1. Competitive Rivalry Relative Risk_____
     a. Top 3 competitors in strategic group:
     b. Firm competitive advantages
     c. Firm competitive disadvantages
     d. Other
   2. Threat of New Entrants Relative Risk _____
     a. Nature of the threat
     b. Recent means of entry by new firms
     c. Competitive Factors attracting new firms
     d. Competitive Factors deterring entrance
     e. Other
   3. Threat of Substitutes Relative Risk _____
     a. Kinds of services or products available
     b. Top 3 competitors
     c. Distinguishing competitive factors (price, time saver, etc.,)
     d. Other

(Continued)

4. Bargaining Power of Suppliers Relative Risk _____
   a. Kinds of products/services provided
   b. Top 3 suppliers
   c. Agreements
   d. Satisfaction ranges
   e. Other

5. Bargaining Power of Buyers Relative Risk _____
   a. Business structures:
   b. Agreements
   c. Satisfaction ranges
   d. Other

6. Opportunities with Complementors Relative Risk _____
   a. Kinds of products/services
   b. Top-3 complementors
   c. Agreements
   d. Other

7. Threat or Cooperation of Other Stakeholders Relative Risk _____
   a. Additional stakeholders
   b. Stakeholders' stakes
   c. Likelihood of cooperation

Conclusion: After determining the relative risk of each driving force to the firm, analyze the collective opportunities and challenges in the industry and identify some strategies and actions the firm can take to strategically address each when rivalry and profits are of concern.

Appendix 15: Table Rows, Columns, and Cells

Column1/Row 1 Column 2	Column 3	Column 4	Column 5
Row 2			
Row 3			
Row 4			

REFERENCES

Abernethy, M. A., & Brownell, P. (1999). The role of budgets in organizations facing strategic change: An exploratory study. *Accounting, Organizations and Society, 24,* 189–204.

Altier, W. J. (1999). *The thinking manager's toolbox: Effective processes for problem solving and decision making.* London: Oxford University Press.

Astley, W. G., & Fombrun, C. J. (1983). Collective strategy: Social ecology of organization environments. *Academy of Management Review, 8*(4), 576–587.

Barney, J. B. (1991). Firm resources and sustained competitive advantage. *Journal of Management, 17*(1), 99–120.

Bertalanffy, L. V. (1950). The theory of open systems in physics and biology, *Science, New Series, 111*(2872), 23–29.

Bertocci, P. A. (1970). *The person God is.* London: Allen and Unwinn.

Burton-Houle, T. (2000). *Field guide to the theory of constraints thinking processes.* New Haven, CT: AGI.

Carroll, A. B. (1979). A three-dimensional conceptual model of corporate social performance. *Academy of Management Review, 4,* 497–505.

Carroll, A. B., & Buchholtz, A. K. (2006). *Business and society ethics and stakeholder management* (6th ed.). Mason, OH: South-Western.

Carter, L. E. (2006). The African American personalist perspective on person as embodied in the life and thought of Martin Luther King Jr. *Speculative Journal of Philosophy, 20*(3), 219–223.

Chesbrough, H. W., & Teece, D. J. (1996). When is virtual virtuous? Organizing for innovation. *Harvard Business Review, 74*(1), 65–73.

Cochran, L. (1997). *Career counseling: A narrative approach.* Thousand Oaks, CA: Sage.

Coras, E., Tantau, L., & Dumitrum, A. (2013). A risk mitigation model in SME's open innovation projects. *Management & Marketing, 8*(2), 303–328.

Coulter, M. K. (2013). *Strategic management in action* (6th ed., 272 pp.). Upper Saddle River, NJ: Pearson Prentice-Hall.

Cox, J. F., III, Blackstone, J. H., Jr, & Schleier, J. G., Jr. (2003). *Managing operations: A focus on excellence*. Great Barrington, MA: North River Press.

Cox, T. (1991). The multicultural organization. *The Executive, 5*(2), 34–47.

Demonstrating Value. (2013). Financial ratio analysis. Retrieved from http://www.demonstratingvalue.org/resources/financial-ratio-analysis

Dess, G. G., Lumpkin, G. T., & Taylor, M. L. (2005). *Strategic management* (2nd ed.). New York, NY: McGraw-Hill Irwin.

de Wit, B., & Meyer, R. (2002). *Strategy synthesis: Resolving strategy paradoxes to create competitive advantage*. London: Thomson.

Dhingra, N., Samo, A., Schaninger, B., & Schrimper, M. (2021). Help your employees find purpose – Or watch them leave. Retrieved from https://www.mckinsey.com/business-functions/people-and-organizational-performance/our-insights/help-your-employees-find-purpose-or-watch-them-leave

Draman, R. H., & Edmondson, V. C. (2012). Why a new approach is needed to solve today's business problems: A narrative review. *Review of Management Innovation and Creativity, 5*(14), 88–104.

Drucker, P. F. (1967). *The effective executive*. London: Heinemann.

Duquia, R. P., Bastos, J. L., Bonamigo, R. R., González-Chica, D. A., & Martínez-Mesa, J. (2014). Presenting data in tables and charts. *Anais Brasileiros de Dermatologia, 89*(2), 280–285.

Edmondson, B. S., Edmondson, V. C., Adams, J., & Barnes, J. (2020). We challenge you to join the movement: From discourse to critical voice. *Journal of Management Education, 44*(2), 247–266.

Edmondson, V. C. (1996). *After entry, then what? An examination of the strategy and performance of minority-owned ventures in the US construction industry*. Athens, GA: University of Georgia. Dissertation Abstracts International.

Edmondson, V. C. (2022). After entry, then what 25 years later: revisiting Edmondson's typology of competitive strategies of black-owned firms in the U.S. construction industry. Manuscript submitted for publication.

Edmondson, V. C., & Edmondson, B. S. (2017). From critical thinking to critical voicing. Paper presented at Black Lives Matter, Blue Lives Matter Conference, Morehouse College, Atlanta, GA.

Edmondson, V. C., & Munchus, G. (2001). The Atlanta way: A gateway to entry for ethnic business enterprises. *Entrepreneurship Policy Journal, 1*(1), 35–41.

Edmondson, V. C., & Munchus, G. (2007). Managing the unwanted truth: A framework of dissent strategy. *Journal of Organizational Change Management, 20*(6), 747–760.

Edmondson, V. C., & Shannon, J. P. (2020). From critical thinking to critical voicing for impact. *IUP Journal of Soft Skills, 14*(4), 27–45.

Edmondson, V. C., Zebal, M., Bhuiyan, M., Crumbly, J., & Jackson, F. H. (2021). Help yourself by lifting up someone else: The promise of entrepreneurship ecosystems for black Americans in the U.S. Manuscript submitted for publication.

Fine, A., & Merrill, R. (2010). *You already know how to be great: A simple way to remove interference and unlock your greatest potential.* New York, NY: Portfolio Penguin.

Fuson, K. C., Kalchman, M., & Bransford, J. D. (2005). Mathematical understanding: An introduction. In M. S. Donovan & J. Bransford (Eds.), *How students learn mathematics in the classroom* (pp. 217–256). Washington, DC: National Research Council.

Gamble, J. E., Thompson, A. A., & Peteraf, M. A. (2013). *Essentials of strategic management: The quest for competitive advantage* (3rd ed.). Irwin, CA: McGraw-Hill.

Garcea, N., Isherwood, S., & Linley, A. (2011). Do strengths measure up? *Strategic Human Resources Review, 10*(2), 5–11.

Goldratt, E. M. (1990). *Theory of constraints.* Croton-on-Hudson, NY: North River Press.

Goldratt, E. M. (1994). *It's not luck.* Great Barrington, MA: North River Press.

Goldratt, E. M., & Cox, J. (1984). *The goal.* Croton-on-Hudson, NY: North River Press.

Goold, M., & Campbell, A. (1998). Desperately seeking synergy. *Harvard Business Review, 76*(5), 131–143.

Grove, A. S. (1996). *Only the paranoid survive.* New York, NY: Doubleday.

Guffey, M. E., & Loewy, D. (2018). *Business communication: Process and product* (9th ed.). Boston, MA: Cengage.

Hickson, D. J., Butler, R. J., Cray, D., Mallory, G. R., & Wilson, D. C. (1986). *Top decisions: Strategic decision making in organizations* (pp. 26–42). San Francisco, CA: Jossey-Bass.

Lan, J. (2012). [CE6]16 Financial ratios for analyzing a company's strengths and weaknesses. *American Association of Individual Investors Journal.* Retrieved from 16-financial-ratios-for-analyzing-a-companys-strengths-and-weaknesses.pdf

Malik, R. F. (2015). *Turning up the volume: How executive coaches use assessment tools to inform their coaching process.* PhD thesis, University of Georgia, Athens, GA.

Malik, R. F., Gupte, G., Edmondson, B., & Edmondson, V. C. (2017). Building consumer competence and trust: HRD professionals as champions of change. *Journal of the North American Management Society, 11*(1), 9–21.

Mankin, J. A., & Jewell, J. J. (2014). A sorry state of affairs: The problems with financial ratio education. *Academy of Education Leadership Journal*, *18*(4), 195–219.

Miles, R. E., & Snow, C. C. (1978/2003). *Organizational strategy, structure, and process*. Palo Alto, CA:Stanford University Press.

Mintzberg, H. (1987). The strategy concept 1: Five Ps for strategy. *California Management Review*, *30*(1), 11–24.

Moore, J. F. (1993). Predators and prey: A new ecology of competition. *Harvard Business Review*, *71*(3), 75–83.

Neumeyer, X., Santos, S. C., & Morris, M. H. (2019). Who is left out: Exploring social boundaries in entrepreneurial ecosystems? *Journal of Technology Transfer*, *44*(2), 462–484.

North, T. T. (2012). *Forensic leadership: Changing the culture of a nation*. Bloomington, IN: Authorhouse.

Pinker, S. (2016). North. Retrieved from http://theweek.com/articles/639004/how-better-writer-6-tips-from-master-linguist

Porter, M. E. (1979). How competitive forces shape strategy. *Harvard Business Review*, *59*(2), 137–145.

Porter, M. E. (1980). *Competitive strategy: Techniques for analyzing industries and competitors*. New York, NY: Free Press.

Pounds, W. F. (1969). The process of problem finding. *Industrial Management Review*, *10*(1), 1–19.

Thomas, D. A., & Ely, R. J. (1996). Making differences matter. A new paradigm for managing diversity. *Harvard Business Review*, *74*(5), 79–90.

Thompson, A., Strickland, A., & Gamble, J. (2008). *Crafting and executing strategy: The quest for competitive advantage*. New York, NY: McGraw-Hill.

Thurman, H. (1998). The public and private results of collegiate education in the life of Negro Americans. In W. Fluker & C. Tumber (Eds.), *Strange freedom: The best of Howard Thurman on religious experience and public life* (pp. 160–162). Boston, MA: Beacon Press.

United States Department of Health and Human Services Competency Framework. (n.d.). Retrieved from https://hhsu.learning.hhs.gov/competencies/core-decision_making.asp

United States Security Exchange Commission (n.d.). Retrieved from https://www.sec.gov/. Accessed on April 5, 2022.

Wells, C., Malik, R. F., & Edmondson, V. C. (2021). The influence of diversity climate on employer branding: 2020 and beyond. *IUP Journal of Brand Management*, *18*(1), 32–47.

Wheelen, T. L., & Hunger, J. D. (2012). *Strategic management and business policy: Toward global sustainability* (13th ed.). Upper Saddle River, NJ: Pearson Prentice-Hall.

GLOSSARY

10K An annual report filed with the US Securities and Exchange Commission (SEC) that provides a detailed picture of a company's business, the risks it faces, and the operating and financial results for a fiscal year.

Accepted risk The willingness to take on the risk of a potential problem and its likely causes, thus removing it from further consideration in the planning process.

Acquisition The purchase of a company by another company.

Activity A part of an action plan that will be undertaken by an individual or team.

Analysis paralysis A state of indecision as a result of seeking the perfect strategy.

Annual report A document published each year by a company to show its leadership, financial performance, and portfolio of products.

Appendix The end of a report that includes additional information for the decision makers' perusal if desired.

Banana A circle used to connect conditions within a necessity clause in a Current Reality Tree.

Bankruptcy A retrenchment strategy that seeks to have a court assist with restructuring debts when a company cannot repay creditors as per their contract.

Belonging A feeling that stakeholders have when an organization demonstrates they are valued.

Benchmarking The process of measuring performance in key result areas against those of competitors recognized as industry leaders or another member of your strategic group.

Best practice A procedure that is followed by successful and ethical companies.

Brainstorming The oral process of generating ideas in a group.

Brainwriting The written process of generating ideas as an individual prior to a brainstorming session.

Budget A financial plan used to estimate expenses that will be incurred in implementing the strategy to use available funds wisely.

Business model The mix of activities a company performs to fulfill its mission.

Business strategy   The competitive and cooperative strategies that seek to improve a company's competitive position in an industry or market segment.

Client implementation plan   A plan of action created by a consultant that will be implemented by a client.

Code of ethics   A code that states how an organization expects its contributors to behave and work with others on the job.

Competence   The ability to perform a skill or task in a preferred way.

Competitive strategy   The strategy that states how a company or business unit will compete in an industry against its rivals.

Complementor   A company or industry whose products or services work well with another company's or industry's offerings.

Component   A planned action that will be taken or a person that will be responsible for an action in an implementation plan.

Constraint   An input that places limitations on what can be done by the company to compete.

Contract   A written or spoken agreement that is intended to be enforceable by law.

Contribution   The impact of intentionally collaborating with others to achieve a goal or meet an objective.

Copyright   The protection of original work and the exclusive right to authorize others to use it.

Corporate social responsibility A concern for how a business behaves to have a positive impact in its environment.

Corporate strategy   A strategy that states a company's overall direction when there is more than one strategic business unit.

Corporate visioning   The art of telling your stakeholders who you are through your mission statement, vision statement, logo, slogan, etc.

Correction   An action taken during the implementation stage to remedy something that is not going or has not gone as planned.

Corrective action   An action(s) taken during the implementation stage to lessen the chance that something will continue to go wrong.

Current Reality Tree   A diagram that explains what is going on in an organization (i.e., the strategic issue).

Customer   The person or entity that purchases your product or service; not always the end-user.

Deadline   The latest time that an expectation can be met.

Decision analysis   A research-based effort to identify (e.g., select, determine, or develop) a strategy to improve the current reality.

Decision situation   A situation when decision making is unavoidable.

Department implementation plan   A plan of action that will be implemented by contributors in one or more departments within an organization.

Deviation   A change from what was planned versus what actually occurred.

Digital technology   A type of technology that leads to an interactive experience.

Diversity   A strategic human resource strategy that values individual differences and group similarities.

Divestment   A retrenchment or turnaround strategy where strategic business units are sold.

Downsizing   A human resource strategy that involves the planned elimination of people or positions.

Duty of care   An ethical concern for people over profits.

End-user   The person or entity at the end of the supply chain that uses a finished product.

Engagement letter   A letter that details the scope of activities that will be undertaken by the contributors on a project and what is needed from each party to be successful.

Equality   The perspective that diverse groups should be treated the same regardless of outcomes.

Equity   The perspective that diverse groups should be treated fairly according to their needs in order to achieve similar group outcomes.

Ethics A rule of conduct that goes beyond what the law requires in decision situations.

Ethical judgment   A decision made by an individual which dictates how he or she behaves in a given situation or overall; and may have severe consequences for the individual and the company.

Evaluation and control   A process in which a company's activities and performance are monitored so that actual performance can be compared with planned performance.

Expectation   The anticipated outcome of an objective or strategy.

Facilitation   The act of providing direction to team members to ensure the strategic process is followed to meet team and organizational objectives most effectively and efficiently.

Failure   An unmet objective that results in an opportunity to learn and try a new approach.

Forecasting   The act of relying on past experiences and information to drive decision making.

Freeride   The act of gaining the benefits of being a member of a team while not fully participating.

Functional analysis   An analysis of one or more of the functional areas of business to determine how decisions align with the current strategy or may affect a proposed strategy.

Functional strategy   The business model within one functional area of business.

Goal   A planned or desired outcome or end-result of a strategy or strategic plan.

Groupthink   A detriment of working in teams and group decision making whereby opportunities to individually contribute are set aside due to a desire for harmony and getting the work done efficiently.

Implementation plan   A document that outlines the rationales, components, and roles recommended for accomplishing objectives set by decision makers

Implementation planning   The act of identifying the components and roles needed to put a strategy into action, including identifying and addressing potential problems and their likely causes

Inclusion   An intentional effort to provide opportunities for diverse members to have visibility and a substantive voice in an organization's decision making

Intellectual property   The rights given to persons over their creations over a certain period of time

Key result areas   The areas deemed important to the success of a strategy and are monitored and tracked as the strategy progresses

Leading   The act of providing direction to team members to use their knowledge, abilities, and skills most effectively and efficiently to achieve team and organizational objectives

Likely cause   A factor that may create a problem during implementation

Liquidation   A retrenchment strategy whereby the company opts to dissolve a business

Merger   A transaction where two or more companies agree to become one through an exchange of stocks or ownership

Mission statement   A formal statement that describes what the company does currently to meet the needs of its customers

Morals The principles that govern right or wrong personal conduct.

Necessity clause   A situation in which more than one condition (i.e., an undesirable effect in a Current Reality Tree) is needed for another condition to occur

New entrants   The firms entering an industry

Objective   A planned or desired outcome of an activity, tactic, component, or strategy

Outsourcing   A process of purchasing products or services from suppliers rather than making or performing them

Participation   The act of working with others to achieve a goal or meet an objective

Patent   A license giving someone or a firm the sole right to make, use, or sell an invention for a set period

Performance   The actual outcome of the strategic management process

Personal identity   A composite of your beliefs, values, abilities, aspirations, personal style, etc., that make you who you are

Players   The decision makers, influencers, and contributors in the strategy making process

Prediction   The act of relying on current experiences and information about the future to drive decision making

Preventive action   An action that is taken during the planning stage to lessen the chance that something will go wrong

Proactive trigger   An action that signals that attention to a tactic is needed to ensure the success of a strategy

Proficiency   The ability to perform an act as expected or demanded

Reactive trigger   A signal that something has happened that requires action

Residual probability   The chance that a preventive action will not accomplish its aim

Resolution strategy visual   A visual that gives stakeholders a glimpse into how a proposed strategy will work and be implemented

Resource   An input that increases the strategic options that can be used by the firm to compete

Resource allocation   The act of identifying and putting resources to use where they are likely to have a positive impact on the strategy

Retrenchment strategy   A plan to improve a company's performance before conditions become dire

Risk   The likelihood that an action will have a negative impact

Scenario planning   A forecasting technique that outlines different outcomes in a narrative

Skill   The ability to perform a task

S.M.A.R.T. performance objectives   The belief that performance objectives should be written using the SMART framework. This means that each performance objective should be specific, measurable, attainable, relevant to the organization's mission, goals, and strategies, and time-bound

Sponsor   A person or organization that recognizes the value of an idea, or another person or organization and is willing to champion and financially support their effort

Stake   An interest, often physical or financial, in a company's outcomes

Stakeholder   A player that can influence or is influenced by a company's strategy

Status report   A report that allows a team to track how well it is meeting its objectives and to identify corrective actions

STEEP or PESTEL analysis   The process of scanning for opportunities and threats in the general environment, specifically, sociocultural, technological, economic, and political–legal factors

Strategic fit   The match between proposed or new decisions and existing decisions

Strategic flexibility   The ability to shift from one strategy to another

Strategic group   A group of firms that are direct competitors pursuing similar strategies in the same industry

Strategic management   A set of management decisions and actions that determines the long-term performance of an organization. Originally called business policy, strategic management incorporates strategic thinking that is used for analysis, strategy formulation, and execution that are employed to lead an organization to sustainable success

Strategic orientation   The approach that determines how a company interacts with its environment to gain a competitive advantage

Strategic type   The categorization of firms based on their strategic orientation

Strategy   A comprehensive approach to how the company will fulfill its mission and achieve its goals

Strategy content   The details of a strategy that will drive the strategy process

Strategy context   The situation in which a company's strategy will be implemented

Strategy formulation   The development of a strategy that is deemed to be able to meet a company's objectives given the context in which it competes

Strategy implementation   The act of putting the strategy into action and adapting as necessary to meet a company's objectives

Strategy process   The details of how the strategy content will be performed

Structure follows strategy   The strategic fit between the organization's strategy and structure, whereby if the strategy changes the structure changes

Substitutes   The products or services from different industries that satisfy the same need

Success   A met objective that results in an opportunity to learn and try a similar if not new approach

Sufficiency clause   A situation in which one condition (i.e., an undesirable effect in a Current Reality Tree) can lead to another

Summary handout   A document that covers the key content discussed in a meeting

SWOT analysis   A three-step process that includes: (1) identifying internal factors (strengths and weaknesses) and external factors (opportunities and threats); (2) strategic options (TOWS matrix); and (3) competitive advantages and disadvantages for a specific company

Tactic   A planned action that is part of a larger strategy to achieve an objective

Talent   The contributors who are involved in the strategic management process at every level

Template   A pre-formatted/predesigned document that was created according to management's instructions that only needs to be updated and saved as the strategy progresses

TOWS matrix   A table that shows how internal and external factors can be matched to show strategic options available to a company

Trademark   A legally recognizable and protected word, phrase, symbol, design, or a combination of these things that differentiates products and services from all others of its kind

Trade secret   The confidential commercially valuable information protected by Intellectual Property laws

Trigger   The point when it is clear the strategy is not going as planned

Turnaround strategy   A plan to improve the company's performance when things are dire

Undesirable effect   A negative consequence of decision making

Visionary   The ability to see the organization for what it can become

Vision statement   A formal statement that describes what the company sees itself becoming in the future

Work identity   The identity that a person presents in the workplace to achieve their career goals.

INDEX

Note: Page numbers followed by "*n*" indicate notes.